AF622098

COURTS AND ADMINISTRATION OF JUSTICE UNDER CHHATRAPATI SHIVAJI

COURTS AND ADMINISTRATION OF JUSTICE UNDER CHHATRAPATI SHIVAJI

T.T. MAHAJAN

Commonwealth

Courts and Administration of
Justice Under Chhatrapati Shivaji

© T.T.Mahajan

ISBN : 81-7169-198-6

Edition : 2027

Published by :
COMMONWEALTH PUBLISHERS (P) LTD.
4831/24, Govind Lane,
Ansari Road, Darya Ganj,
New Delhi - 110002
Ph. : 23272541, 23242541
e-mail : commonwealthpublishers2016@gmail.com

Distributed by :
ARJUN PUBLISHING HOUSE
4831/24, Govind Lane,
Ansari Road, Darya Ganj,
New Delhi - 110002
Ph. : 23272541, 23242541
e-mail : arjunbooks2001@gmail.com

Laser Typesetting by :
Dimple Computers
Delhi

Printed at :
Divine Digital Press
Delhi

DEDICATED TO

Honourable Shri Dadasaheb Shivajirao G. Patil, Ex-Minister for Co-operation and Legislative Affairs, Maharashtra State, Chairman of National Federation Co-op. Sugar Factories, New Delhi, and Indian Sugar and General Industry Export and Import Co-op. Ltd., New Delhi, Director of Maharashtra State Co-op. Sugar Factories Federation Ltd., and Maharashtra State Co-op. Marketing Federation, National Heavy Engg. Co-op. Ltd., Pune, Maharashtra State Co-op. Oil Seeds Growers Federation Ltd., Vice-Chairman, Vasantdada Sugar Institute, Pune, and Chairman of Shirpur Shetkari Sahakari Sakhar Karkhana Ltd. as a token of gratitude and respect for his valuable contribution to the cause of Socio-Economic Development of West Khandesh.

INTRODUCTION

The aim of our study is to depict the judicial organization in Kingdom of Shivaji, as it emerges from original records of the Seventeenth Century. The work throws some new light upon the Chhatrapati's justice without partiality as reflected in his decisions, actions and instructions. It mainly deals with the topics such as characteristic features of judiciary under the rule of Chhatrapati Shivaji, the role of King in settling of the disputes, judicial bodies in his Kingdom, provincial administration of civil and criminal justice, offence and penalty etc. The main cause that can be attributed to the success of Shivaji's judicial administration was the honesty and impartiality. Another noteworthy point that has been discussed fully in the work is the Gotamajlis, a sort of the democratic institution which helped the King not only in administering the justice, but also served as considerable check upon the absolute power of the Maratha : Chhatrapati.

Some scholars who deserve to be mentioned and who have made the first attempt systematically on the work of judiciary under the Marathas are Dr. V.T. Gune and Dr. S.N. Sen. Dr. Gune wrote much more about the judicial system in medieval Maharashtra extending from the period of the Deccan Muslim Sultans to the end of the Peshwa rule. He wrote extensively on the subject and his work covers much wider and long period for the study of the judiciary under the Marathas.

However, some important aspects such as the account of disputes settled by King Shivaji himself in his court, his role as an impartial King of justice and disputable cases actually settled by the judicial courts such as Rajsabha, Subhamajlis, Brahmasabha, Gotasabha in Maratha Kingdom of the Seventeenth Century are still important gaps remained and to be studied by the scholars of Maratha history.

The present study which confines to the Shivaji's period only, helps us to estimate properly the role of Shivaji as an impartial King and the head of the judiciary.

It is hoped, the present work will enable the scholars to have a good insight into an understanding of the judiciary existed in Swaraj under Shivaji's rule. In order to throw full light on the subject, I have given in detail the account of disputes settled by King Shivaji himself and the judicial machinery functioning in his Kingdom. King Shivaji seems to have proud of himself on his love of equity. He regarded the justice as a sacred task and never thought it as an imposed duty. He was not only the Supreme Judge of his Kingdom but the Chief of the highest Majlis too. Any person had permission to approach the King who would listen to the complaints of his subjects and also gave the judgements.

Here in this work an attempt has been made to examine the nature of various types of courts that were in existence in Maratha Kingdom in the 17th Century and also the judicial cases decided by those courts. While studying the records dealing with judicial decisions (Mahzars) of the period under review, one may find how King Shivaji with the help of experts, interpreted the Hindu laws that were in existence in medieval Maharashtra from the ancient times and also observed them strictly when he conducted the State Administration of justice. Like many other rulers in India, in the Maratha Kingdom too, Shivaji was the chief justice. In practice it was difficult for the King to dispense justice personally in every case that came up before him. Hence, a justice was appointed by the King for trying the civil and criminal cases. The Nyayadhish and the Panditrao were generally the judges in Shivaji's Kingdom. Describing the Nyayadhish, King's judge who was present in the court, the contemporary records speak of him as one of the eight ministers of Chhatrapati Shivaji.

The existence of local bodies in territorial divisions like Subha, Pargana, Tarf, Kasba and the village etc., of his Kingdom shows that though King Shivaji personally dispensed justice in some of the important cases, yet, many other disputes were mostly settled by those lower courts. Shivaji very often, asked his superior officers to decide those cases with the help of the Gotasabha brought before them. In some important cases the appeals were taken to the King through the officers like Subhedar, the Deshmukh, the Patil etc.

In the capital town, the court held in person and presided over by King Shivaji to administer the justice, was the Supreme Court of Maratha Kingdom. In the territorial divisions of his State, the lower courts were replaced by the local bodies which exercised several powers. Those lower courts in province were presided over by King Shivaji's officers such as Subhedar, Hawaldar, Deshmukh, Shete Mahajan and the Mokadam etc., who in the name of and on behalf of their Master dispensed justice to the urban and rural folk. Such lower courts which acted as popular courts in jurisdiction of their territorial units decided mostly the civil cases brought before them. Thus, the Subha Majlis or pargana Gotasabha, the Kasba Gotasabha and the Gotasabha of the village etc., were discharging the judicial duties and they were presided over by the Subhedar, the Deshmukh, Shete and Mokadam respectively. The contemporary records reveal that in rare cases, King's officers presiding over the lower courts gave decisions with partiality, it was Shivaji who could make the correct decisions impartially.

I am grateful to the authorities of the Jayakar Library, Pune, Bharat Itihas Sanshodhan Mandal's Library, and the Deccan College Library, Pune for their necessary co-operation and help rendered to me for completing this work.

I am grateful to Annasaheb, V.T. Randhir, the President of K.V.P. Sanstha, Shirpur for his kindness and encouragement. My deep gratitude and appreciation go to Shri S.M. Patel, Principal of our College for his constant inspiration and necessary help.

I am also thankful to Shri D.B. Patil, the librarian and the staff of our library who provided me the library facilities.

I take an opportunity to thank my friends, Shri G.D. Sisode, Prof. P.S. Anturlikar, Prof. G.M. Patil, Prof. M.N. Mali, Prof. S.A. Patil who have shown keen interest in getting this work completed. Indeed, it would have been difficult for me to complete the present work successfully without the help of my daughter Manisha and sons, namely Prashant and Sachin. Finally, my wife, Suman deserves my many cordial thanks for freeing me from some domestic duties. Without her help and co-operation, it would not be possible for me to write this book.

T.T. Mahajan

SOURCES

Marathi Chronicles

In respect of Bakhars as source of present work, it can be stated that though they are not as important as other contemporary records of our period, they also contain some relevant information for our study. Among such Marathi chronicles bearing upon our topic mention may be made to the Sabhasad Bakhar, ninety-one Qalami Bakhar and Srishivdigvijaya etc., which occasionally throw valuable light on important aspects such as the members of the Rajmandal, the heads of territorial units, the names of Shivaji's chief judges, his rules prohibiting the men to capture the women, children of the enemy, some kinds of punishments inflicted upon the criminals etc. The Sabhasad Bakhar and Sridigvijaya are of little relevance to the present study and contain only some pieces of evidences helping us to describe the duties of the King and also the spirit in which King Shivaji administered justice to his people.

Apart from some exaggerated and fantastic statements, those Bakhars serve our useful purpose and throw considerable light on King Shivaji's attitude towards impartial justice. Sabhasad Bakhar which supplies us an authentic account, also describes the qualities to be possessed by the good judges. Tarikhe Shivaji, the Persian Chronicle is another source of our study which furnishes useful information on various fines imposed on the offenders by the king.

Sanskrit Sources

Dandaniti : Of much importance particularly for the chapters like offence and penalty in present work is the *Dandaniti*, the Sanskrit work of Kesava Pandit dealing with some aspects of our subject. The work is divided into six chapters throwing light on topics such as danda, offences, adultery, rape, defamation, assaults etc. Kesava Pandit gives much information and guidance to administer the criminal justice of the Maratha period. The author of the work had received favour and patronage of King Shivaji.[1] The period of composition of the work has been stated in between 1681 and 1683 A.D. He presented the copy of the work to Chhatrapati Sambhaji on the occasion of his ascendancy to the throne.[2] The text contains valuable information about the assembly of learned scholars called by King Shivaji in 1664 A.D. at Rajapur to decide the dispute arose between Golawalikar Pandhyes and Devarukhe Brahmins regarding the rights of Syenavis.[3] Kesava Pandit describes various crimes prevailed in Maharashtra and in other parts of India of the medieval period. Hence, the Sanskrit text is much useful for knowing the information about the administration of criminal jurisprudence of Maratha Kingdom of the Seventeenth Century.

Sukranitisara is essentially a work on polity of Sukracharya, a theorist of medieval period. His work is much useful for our study since it reflects contemporary procedure resembling the judicial practice followed during Shivaji's period. It, while describing judicial procedure of medieval times, refers to Sabha Naik or Adhyaksha and Mahaprashnik. The work throws some light on methods of punishment like mutilation and various types of danda to be inflicted upon the criminals. The work amply furnishes valuable information for the present study of the practice of granting Jayapatra to the winner. The author gives us an insight into various duties to be performed by the King. For the purpose of our study the English translation of the work given in Sacred Books of the East, Vol. VII, has been used.

Documents of Historical Families

The Itihasacharya V.K. Rajwade has edited and published many documents relating to some historical families of Shivaji's period such as the Deshpande family of Supe and Shirwal, the Jadhav family of Umbaraj, Dharmadhikari of Kolhapur, Joshi of Kalyan and Puntambe, Aradhya of Pandharpur etc., under the head of Marathyanchya Itihasachi Sadhane in volume number VIII, XV, XVI, XVII and XX etc. The study of those documents helps us for knowing various judicial judgements declared by King Shivaji, the Brahmasabha and the Gotamajlis of the village. Some of those documents also throw considerable light on the working of the judicial machinery prevailed in the parganas and prants of the Maratha Kingdom. In addition to above mentioned records, the documents which are of more relevance to our study constitute a number of family papers belonging to the Desai of Dharwad, Koppal, Kudal Lakshmeshwar, the documents of the Deshpande of Shirwal, Supe, Akole, the papers of the Deshmukh of Khedebare, Kudal etc., have been edited and published by K.V. Purandare, D.V. Potdar, Majumdar, S.N. Joshi, G.H. Khare under the title Shiv Charitra Sahitya in parts one to thirteen, the series of BISM Poona. Some of those documents are the Mahzars i.e. the verdicts given by majlis on the disputes of the Mokadami Watan, the Deshmukhi Watan, Joshi-Kulkarni Watan or Mahar Vritti etc. The detailed description of the Gota decision, the Brahmasabha, the procedure of the decision by the majlis, the judicial functions of Government officials in province, kinds of crime of murder, punishments, the nature of Hazir Majlis etc., provides us with much valuable information regarding the judicial bodies during the rule of Chhatrapati Shivaji. To the above mentioned category of the documents, we can add the papers of the Deshpande of Taluka Khedebare or Shivkalin Deshpande's Karina.

Those documents along with other papers have been edited and published by K.V. Purandare under the title Purandare Daftar, Part III, the series of BISM, Poona. The study of their contents reveals that they have much to do with the nature, structure of the Gotamajlis, procedure of the judicial cases, the judicial functions of King's officers like the Deshmukh, Hawaldar etc. Indeed, those papers help us to understand very basically King Shivaji's conception of "Dharma" and "Adharma".

Documents selected from Jamav

Some papers from Jamav section have been published, under the title "Records of the Shivaji's period" by V.G. Khobrekar in 1974. A few of them give us the details about the judgement of King Shivaji and the Gota on the disputes.

Ajnapatra : This work of Ramchandra Pant Amatya gives us very little but valuable information for our study. Ramchandra Amatya who served King Shivaji brought out this work in 1716 A.D., during the reign of Chhatrapati Sambhaji the second of Kolhapur on the request made by the latter.[4] It throws some light on judicial duties of Maratha Chhatrapati, his responsibility of investigating of what was just and unjust etc.

REFERENCES & FOOTNOTES

1. Bendrey V.S., Kesava Pandit's Dandaniti, P. 26
2. Ibid
3. Ibid, PP. 30-31
4. Sen S.N., ASM, P. 3

CONTENTS

ABBREVIATIONS

AP	Ajna Patra
ASM	Administrative System of the Marathas
CSP	Chhatrapati Shivaji Maharajanchi Patre
JSM	Judicial System of the Marathas
MIS	Marathyanchya Itihasachi Sadhane
NHM	New History of the Marathas
PUD	Purandare Daftar
RS	Records of Shivaji Period
SCS	Shiv Charitra Sahitya
SPSS	Shivkalin Patrasar Sangarah
SHT	Shivaji and His Times

1

Characteristic Features of Shivaji's Policy towards Justice

SCOPE OF CHHATRAPATI SHIVAJI'S JUDICIARY

Though King Shivaji was the head of the Maratha State, his judicial powers were not unlimited and unrestricted. His judicial administration was based on the principles of Hindu Laws and Smriti books. King's judicial power was limited by permitting some local judicial bodies to administer the justice. Like other Hindu Kings, Shivaji also did not make the new laws. He did not only observe the principles or rules laid down by the Dharma Shastras and other Smriti Karas, but also followed them when decided the social and individual disputes in the kingdom. Rajsabha (Rajmandal) was a noteworthy body which held the check on King's powers. The Maratha King always administered the justice to his men by consulting this judicial body.

According to the principles laid down by the Dharma Shastras, King Shivaji being the head of the judiciary, possessed unlimited judicial powers, overall kinds of civil and criminal cases of dispute. Actually, some restrictions were imposed on the judicial powers of the Maratha King by appointing the local judicial bodies in the state. The religious disputes were tried by the Dharmadhikari. Panditrao who gave verdict according to the rules laid down by the Dharmashastras, also investigated the religious disputes. In fact, Subha Majlis, Pargana Gota, village Gota etc., i.e. the local assemblies, enjoyed the judicial powers and decided every kind of suit arising in the pargana as well we in the village. Only the judicial decisions regarding the serious offences like killing the person, committing the dacoity etc., were examined and finally decided by the king himself. In his work of judiciary, the king was assisted by the Nyayadhish and other State officials. A large number of cases of crime seem to have decided by the Gotasabhas, or the majlis in the province. Thus, the common people in Maratha society in the 17th Century, had also the share in conducting the Government's business of administration.

Conception of Justice in Hindu Dharmashastras

The need for the State's judicial machinery arose because the men wanted to safeguard their wealth from thieves and robbers. The people in society felt the necessity for the judicial administration for deciding various kinds of disputes and also for inflicting the punishment on the persons doing evil deeds. The Hindu Dharma Shastras stressed on the necessity for king's administration for affording protection to the weaker groups against the strong and evil souls in society. Manu Smriti has laid a stress on king's council of justice by explaining that "Let the king decide the suits of men. If the king does not personally investigate the suits then, let him appoint a learned Brahman to try them".[1] Narad Samhita also points out the administration of justice by referring to the idea that "the king is the fountain-head of justice." The text of the same Samhita further emphasises the assistance of the chief judge by mentioning that let the king try the cases in due order by consulting his chief justice[2]. Brihadaranyaka Upanishad[3] lays considerable stress on law and justice. It says, "the law is the king of the king", he should not divert from it. To Manu,[3-a] "justice consists in decision that is in due accordance with law and is in keeping with the peculiarities of time, place" etc.

Shivaji's Conception of Justice

The reign of King Shivaji brought prosperity, security and organized form of Government for maintaining law and order in Maratha Kingdom in the seventeenth century. Shivaji's idea of justice may be gathered from his letters addressed to the Governors, local officers of his Swaraj territory. The instructions in those letters are certainly the directives of how King Shivaji wanted the judicial heads at local level to dispense justice to his subjects. In one of his letters written to his officers of mamale Dabhol, Shivaji made it clear that the king and his officers should act as the guardian of their subjects.[4] He believed in the principle that justice is the base of the benevolent state. He often prohibited the officers from committing harassment and injustice towards his people.

The king was deadly against the favouriteness shown by the local judicial authorities towards one of the parties involved in the dispute. Favourness was regarded crime that was subject to the king's punishment.[5] Shivaji warned the officers not to be partial to any one of their associates or relatives. If the officer committed injustice by showing partiality to some one, the king would never fail in inflicting him the punishment.[6] King Shivaji was really much enthusiastic about the proper justice. He wanted to have true justice done in every case of disputes. He like an experienced ruler had recognised the importance of true justice in the administration. So he was always active to see that his officials should not be failed in maintaining the proper justice in territories under their jurisdiction. In his enthusiastic spirit for true justice, Shivaji believed that the king was the supreme in administration of State. There is no exaggeration in saying that he never liked or tolerated the interference of local officer in judicial affairs. King Shivaji was careful to see that the officers of local units should not commit any act of injustice while conducting State administration. This attitude is clearly reflected in some of his letters addressed to his officials. Narhari Babaji, the tarfdar of Jalgaon, caused oppression to Suryaji Dunduskar of the village Palghar in 1675 A.D. The woman of his servant committed adultery when she was employed on the work of construction of buildings on the fort of Raigad. Narhari Babaji, the officer considered the woman as guilty and wanted to punish her by collecting from her fifty-seven rupees as fine. The woman was a maid servant of Suryaji Dunduskar. Therefore, with an aim of collecting the amount of fine, king's officers dispatched some sepoys at his house. When Shivaji came to know about the oppressive action taken by the officer, he at once ordered Shamaji Awaji, the Hawaldar of the tarf, to issue instruction to the tarfdar to withdraw the sepoys from Suryaji's house. The king strictly warned the officer that it was not his business to interfere in the case. The case would be decided by the king himself. He also made him aware of his duty that the tarfdar was only to inform the king about the offence committed by the criminals under his jurisdiction.[7]

The contents of the letter reflect the spirit for true justice in which Shivaji wanted his officers to act. It also reveals how Shivaji desired to avoid the tyrannical measures or oppressiveness of his officials and wanted them to practise the righteousness and truthfulness in the administration of justice. Speaking of king's duty towards justice, Shivdigvijay gives following directions to the head of the judicial administration. "If the king punishes those who do not deserve for crime and if he does not offer punishments to those who deserve punishments, such a King never becomes happy in his life and he while living on the earth, takes an experience of sorrowful life of hell.[8] While conducting the administration, the King shall not forget that evil person is his (King's) enemy and wiseman is his friend. The King should always be alert to see that he is not partial to his kins, the wealthy men or the persons born in highly respected families. The King has to conduct the business of justice with honesty. He should investigate those complicated cases which came up to him and find out the truth very skilfully with his intelligency.[9]

Thus, the contents in Shivdigvijaya, well reflect the spirit in which King Shivaji administered justice. It also reflects Shivaji's attitude of impartiality towards justice. It summarises the traditional practices prevailed in Maratha Kingdom and the judicial duties those were assigned by the Dharmashastras to King Shivaji. Ajnapatra also describes the judicial duties performed by the King and were as given below. "The King is responsible for the just and unjust which could happen in his territory. His duty is to administer justice according to laws to promote the welfare of the people,[9-a] to protect his subjects and punish the offenders as per the principles guided by the Dharmashastras. King's responsibility is to investigate into what is just and what is unjust".[10] Another worthy work which provides much information on judicial administration of the criminal cases in Swaraj under Shivaji is the Dandaniti of Kesava Pandit. Referring to the King's care for criminal justice, Dandaniti sheds a flood of light on criminal procedure followed by King Shivaji and his son, Sambhaji. It gives various types of Danda, kinds of crimes, criminals etc., prevailed in Maratha country, during the 17th century.[11]

SHIVAJI'S WORD "DHARMA" SIGNIFIES CORRECT JUSTICE

In the document known as "Karina" of the Deshpande and Deshkulkarni Watan of Khedebare pargana of Shivaji's reign, the word Dharma has been used for correct justice. In that Karina, the Plaintiff Sakho Bhikaji had made an appeal to King Shivaji that his watan and villages had been confiscated from him. In his request, the word "Dharma" has been used. Here he had requested the King to act according to the Dharma which signifies King's act for correct justice. He made an appeal to the King to issue an order to the Deshmukh of the Pargana asking him to transfer the suit to some other place for correct justice.[12] Thus, here, King Shivaji's act of issuing an order to the officer for the transference of the case to other place was regarded as an act of Dharma or the righteous act or King's act for correct justice.

The word Dharma occurring at other place in the same document has much wider meaning than simple law. The Karina contains in detail the cause of dispute on Deshkulkarni Watan during the rule of Shivaji. The plaintiff has given a detailed account of the disputed case. It appears from the information contained in the Karina that while making the conversation with the men of Chimnaji Bapuji, King Shivaji had used the word Dharma as righteous act or the act of truthfulness or lawful act. While speaking about the act of Sakho Bhikaji, the King replied that "He (Sakho Bhikaji) was acting according to the Dharma". But regarding the act of Chimnaji Bapuji the King said, "his act to deny to go to other place for hearing the correct justice was contrary to Dharma" and it was an indication of his falseness.[13] Thus, there, the word Dharma was applied for the righteous act of the person for proper justice. The judicial local bodies such as Subha Gota, Gota of Kasba, village Gota etc., which were similar to the modern democratic organization and assisted King Shivaji in the judicial function, were a prominent feature of King's court of justice.

The Majlis or Gota pargana, Gota of Tarf or Gota of village, etc., all bodies were associated with the State officials, (Rajmudra), the King and they extended full co-ordination with that of King Shivaji.[14] The Maratha King is often found as attending the Gotamajlis and paying respects to the decisions given by them. It is thus quite clear that the Gota majlis was highly respectable body in which the men from all classes such as watandars, Deshaks, Khoom, mirasis, uparis, balutas in villages and parganas, got their presentation while hearing the verdict on the grievances. All those representatives were required to act as witnesses and also to countersign the judicial judgements declared by the majlis. King Shivaji became popular as an observer for strict impartiality in giving justice to his people.

Of the most noteworthy features of Shivaji's administration of justice was that his rule became known for the efficient, impartial and benevolent Government of his age. Some of the letters issued by Shivaji to his officers contain the instructions[15] regarding the treatment to be given to the rayat. Those instructions are the guiding principles of his administration which appropriately expected that the Government officials should not oppress the subjects. But they should observe strict impartiality in administering the justice to them. The credit for the impartiality undoubtedly goes to King Shivaji due to the fact that he never interfered in the matter of the justice of local bodies and executed their decisions by ordering the Government machinery for their implementations. King's attitude of impartial justice and the spirit in which he gave judgements are clearly reflected in some of his letters addressed to his local officers of the pargana. King Shivaji wanted to have proper justice done in all the cases.

Justice without Favour

Other notable characteristic of Shivaji's court of justice was that it gave judgements without favour and fear. The King never allowed his officials or closer persons to interfere in State administration. If any government official indulged in committing an offence necessary action was taken by the King very soon.

For this purpose, he had instructed to his officers like Naroba Mutalik who was the Deshmukh, the head of the Gotasabha of the pargana. The officer of pargana Pune pronounced the judgement on the dispute of Patil Watan of mauje Hadapsar, in favour of Sonaji Tupa and against Rayaji Patil. King Shivaji came to know of the special favour which the Deshmukh showed towards Sonaji Tupa.

He made an enquiry of the case and asked the officer as to why he showed favour to one of the parties ? The King also criticised officer's partial judgement by instructing him that the Deshmukh had no need to administer such partial justice. As soon as Shivaji noticed the favouritism of the officer, he immediately and without hesitation passed an order to him to refund the amount to the concerned person.[16]

Finally, the King issued him an order to refund the amount which he received. At the same time Shivaji also instructed the pargana officer that such dispute would be decided by the King at the court on Raygad. The King asked his officer to inform both the parties to be present before him for hearing the final judgement.[17] Shivaji further warned the Deshmukh that he would not commit any mischievous act of oppression thereafter. Thus, the letter addressed by Shivaji to the Deshmukh clearly reflects the spirit in which the King wanted to administer justice. It also reveals how Shivaji was careful to see that in the local administration of justice, the head of pargana unit should not show any partiality in deciding the cases of disputes. Shivaji could succeed in establishing a well organization of justice in his State due to the fact that he always considered the King as the protector and executor of law and never tried to rule out the decisions taken by the judicial bodies.

Any relative of King's family while conducting the administration of province, if found indulged in bribery, he was severely punished. Sambhaji Mohite, relative of the King was the officer of Supe prant. He involved in bribery by accepting seventy-five hons for conferring the Kulkarni watan on his favourite. The Kulkarni watan of Pandarkar brothers of mauje Kolhale in Supe prant was purchased by Timaji Khanderao for twenty hons in 1657 A.D. Thereafter Pandarkar brothers wanted to repurchase that watan from Timaji Khanderao by repaying the amount of twenty hons to him. But Timaji was not willing to do so. Hence Pandarkar brothers offered seventy-five hons to Sambhaji

Mohite, the hawaldar of Supe prant. The officer tried to persuade Timaji to hand over the watan of Kulkarni to Pandarkar brothers. Sambhaji Mohite tried to compel the person for selling the watan to the earlier party. The officer had harassed Timaji and took away the Kulkarni watan forcibly by beating him severely. The Hawaldar finally sent him into prison for three months. When he was kept in confinement, the officer compelled him to write a document regarding the sale of Kulkarni watan from Timaji for twenty-five hons only. Under severe pressure of the officer, Timaji, the prisoner had no other alternative than to accept twenty hons as the price of watan. But later on the prisoner was released from the confinement. Then he made a complaint regarding the Watan to King Shivaji and brought that report to his notice.[18] The King without hesitation summoned both the parties and the officer of the Subha in his presence. The King very seriously heard the complaint especially regarding the misconduct and oppressiveness of the officer towards the complaint. Finally, King Shivaji, after investigating into the matter with the help of Gotasabha, gave decision in favour of Timaji Khanderao who got his Kulkarni watan thereafter. Before closing the discussion regarding King's judicial decision on above case, it seems necessary to emphasize on the investigation of the allegations of oppressive attitude levelled against the officer. The King held the judicial trial in the popular court. It is interesting to note that Shivaji who very fairly and fearlessly conducted the process of investigation found the hawaldar, one of the members of the relatives of the royal family as guilty. As a result of an investigation Sambhaji Mohite was deposed from his office[19] and his watan was also confiscated by the King. Thus, it shows that King Shivaji administered justice without favour and enforced the judgement of the Gotasabha fearlessly.

Justice without Fear (or Stern Justice)

Next noteworthy feature of Shivaji's judicial court was that it administered justice fearlessly and that too with no favour. Many examples of King's impartial justice may be found in the contemporary records. But a few of them can be cited in the following discussion. In regard to his fearless justice, it can be noted that neither the officer of high rank nor any one of King's kins or associates could create any little hesitation in his mind in announcing the correct judgements of the criminal cases. The most striking instance of Shivaji's justice without favour and fearless judgement is certainly the case of Sakhuji Gaikwad who seems to have been his brother-in-law, a relative of one of the King's wives belonging to the Gaikwad family.[20] Sakhuji Gaikwad, one of the army officers of higher rank was accused for wicked deed of dishonouring the Desai woman.[21] The complaint was lodged with King Shivaji against Sakhuji Gaikwad, who committed rape on Desai woman. She was defeated by the Maratha troops in the battle near Belwadi and was captured. When she was kept in confinement on the fort under the protection of Sakhuji Gaikwad, the latter dishonoured her by performing the evil deed.[22] On hearing the report of the wicked act of Sakhuji, King Shivaji held his trial. The complainant could produce necessary and substantial evidences in her support. After making necessary investigation, the King, therefore, decided to imprison the guilty in the village of Mansuli.[23] The King did not become satisfied with this sort of punishment to be given to the accused. He immediately gave an order to his officer that the eyes of the offender should be put out and the criminal would be kept in prison till the death.[24]

Another ideal example of Shivaji's justice without fear and favour was his decision on the complaint against Babaji Bhikaji Gujar, the Mokadam of mauje Ranje. The headman of Ranje misbehaved with a lady in the village. King Shivaji issued an order to summon the Mokadam for trial in presence of the Gotasabha. The King tried the person with the help of the local body on the allegation of his evil deed. After hearing the case, and examining necessary evidences of the witnesses against the accused, Shivaji announced his judgement in this case. He punished him by confiscating his watan of Mokadam and also issued an order to his officer to cut off the hands and feet of the guilty officer.[25] The modal evidences mentioned above reveal that the relatives of King Shivaji's wife or the state officials of higher rank could never escape, out of favour, from the punishment by Shivaji, nor did they cause any fear in his mind for administering the correct and impartial justice. Shivaji, a fearless and powerful king alone could hold trial of the accused relatives and dared to dismiss them from the state services or punished them very severely when the allegations levelled against them proved to be true.

High and Low Caste Men equal before Dharma (Law)

Among many disputes a case of high caste person and member of low caste family was brought in King's court for judgement. Jagtap and Nilkanthrao Katkar who were born in higher caste, had done injustice on the men of Dhangar (Shepherd) family. The dispute of Patil watan of mauje Supe was the case of the enmity between Shepherd's people and Katkar family and Jagtap. In the year 1676 A.D. Ramoji and Khandoji Jagtap claimed the Patil watan of the village. With the consultation of the Subha Officer, they imprisoned the members of the Shepherd's family.[26] Thus, the local officer of the King supported the cause of men of higher caste family by doing injustice on the members of Dhangar community by sending them into the prison. Therefore, Shepherd's men went to King Shivaji and complained against Katkar and Jagtap. After hearing the details of the dispute regarding the Patil watan, the King became furious out of anger for the injustice made towards the men of lower caste family. Shivaji immediately issued an order to Ragho Ballal, the Subhedar of Junnar, asking him to release the Shepherd's men from prison. The behaviour of the officer was really an act of injustice.

Therefore, the King warned the officer that such dispute would be decided by the King himself. He also informed Katkar and Jagtap to remain present before the King's court for reporting him their conviction. Shivaji wanted to declare the final judgement on this dispute because while giving the decision, the King or law does not accept any distinction between high and low caste people. In King's eyes, high or low men were equal. In the instructions issued to the local officer, Shivaji while emphasizing the King's supremacy, showed that justice cannot be administered for the sake of the dignity of the people of high status. The King seems to have observed strictly that the law is equal to all the cases.[27] An instance of his impartial justice or how he applied the same law impartially to all his officers without any distinction based on caste, religion or rank, is obvious from the punishment given by Shivaji to Deshkulkarni of mamle Cheul. The revenue officer of Cheul failed to keep the detailed account of revenue receipts of the villages. He, thus, made an attempt to defraud the Government by misappropriating the revenue collection. In 1656, when King Shivaji realised his practice, he severely condemned the officer and pronounced that Deshkulkarni was guilty of defalcation of public money. Therefore, the King issued an order to punish the officer by confiscating of his watan.[28]

All men of high and low caste were equal before the law and the person born in high caste if found accused of his misconduct, should not be escaped from the hands of law only because he is born in higher caste. This ideal principle of justice is clearly suggested in one of King Shivaji's letters issued to the officer of Subha Prabhaval. In that letter, Shivaji has warned the officer that the servants like Jivaji Vinayak (a Brahman officer) should be severely and promptly punished for their misconduct. By instructing him further, the King made the Subhedar aware of the principle that he should not be under the impression that the officer would not be punished only because of his being Brahman.[29]

Thus, the contents of the letter reveal that Shivaji wanted to make a Brahman officer realised that before the law all men of high or low caste were equal. It also suggests that Shivaji while administering the justice to his subjects paid attention to equality of all castes in justice and gave punishments to the offenders without considering their caste as a factor for deciding the social disputes.

Justice without taking Position or Designation of the Offender into Account

King Shivaji while administering strict justice never cared for the social status and position of the criminals. When the Patil of the village in tarf Khedebare committed the offence of adultery, the King at once ordered that the offender should be punished by cutting off his hands and legs. Similarly, when Sambhaji Mohite was tried on the allegations levelled against him and was found as offender, the king immediately ordered to confiscate his Watan and property and finally sent him into the prison.[31] These instances illustrate Shivaji's policy of justice. They throw an ample light on the fact that while administering strict justice or while inflicting punishments to the offenders, he did not care for their social status or the designation they acquired.

No Confinement without Proper Trial

Other peculiar feature of Shivaji's judiciary was that no person was to be imprisoned without proper trial. There was no wonder that the King himself used to administer justice when the situation demanded. The Government officials or judicial authorities were instructed by King Shivaji that any person should not be kept in confinement without the completion of the investigation or proper trial of the case. For instance, Ragho Ballal, the Subhedar of prant Junnar was instructed by Shivaji that Ramoji Jagtap, with the help of the Patil of Mauje Supe, seized the men of Dhangar caste without making their enquiry and sent them into the prison. The king brought into the notice of the officer, that if he behaved like this, his acts would cause to the displeasure of his master. Therefore, the king issued him a letter containing strict warning that the officer possessed no right to confine the persons without taking their offence into consideration. The king gave an order to the Subhedar to release the men of Dhangar community immediately and also instructed him that the dispute between Jagtap and Dhangar would be finally decided by the king personally and he should not interfere into the case unnecessarily.[32] Next remarkable feature of King Shivaji's judicial system was that the disputes were decided at holy places or in public places of worship. The majlis held its meetings in temples of goddesses of Ganapati or Shiva[33] or the Khandoba[34] in the village or on the banks of rivers or at the confluence of two sacred rivers. The Marathas also worshipped the spot where two or more rivers met each other. The rivers and holy places were selected for deciding the cases because it was expected that the witness could speak the truth when he was asked to be present at those sacred places for giving the evidences.

Corruption Regarded an Offence

Shivaji had established his sway over all the provisions of his kingdom. The king followed almost all forms of justice. He laid stress on the corruption as a crime. To check the crime, the act of receiving bribe from one party was regarded crime. Moreover, to corrupt the State officials, servants, judicial authority at local level or at the centre, etc., was also considered as an offence. For instance, a Subhedar of Supe prant when found involved in accepting bribe was declared as an offender and was punished by King Shivaji. His property or Watan was confiscated by the king and he was sent into the prison too. Likewise, Pandarkar brothers who tried to corrupt the governor were also regarded as criminal from whom the Maratha Government collected five hundred hons as the penalty for crime.

Trial by King Shivaji in person at the Royal Court or at Open Place

The most peculiar feature of Shivaji's system of administration of justice was that he used to administer justice and also hear appeals at the royal court on Rayagad and also at open places like temples in villages. It appears from the contemporary records of Shivaji's period that the king was personally leading to the temple of the goddess like Khandoba at Pali and decided the dispute between Kharade and Kalbhor.[36] He used to decide such cases personally with the assistance of Gota majlis or with the help of judicial officer at local level. On such occasions, every officer of the Government had to be present before the king. But the criminal cases like committing adultery etc. were to be decided personally by the king.[37] The offender was presented by the king in the court for trial. The Nyayadhish and the Panditrao in council attended the court and assisted the king in announcing the judgements on disputes.

Equality of Treatment of the Muslims with the Hindus in Legal Rights and Status

Talking of the equal treatment and position of the Muslims in Shivaji's kingdom, it can be said that he had followed the principle of equality of the treatment of the Muslims with the Hindus in legal rights. The king had conferred legal rights over the Inam lands to the Muslims as well as to the Hindus in his state. For instance, Shivaji had continued the Inam of one chavar land to the Muslim persons like Shaikh Abdulla in Poona Pargana.[38] He had also conferred the legal rights over some Inam lands on the Muslims in Pune, Indapur, Chakan Supe, Baramati and also in such other parganas in his territory.[39] He never allowed his officials to confiscate the lands belonging to the Muslims on the ground that they were not the followers of Hinduism. King Shivaji made no distinction of religious faith in employing the Muslims in State services. Under his rule, the Muslim men like Daulatkhan[40] and Nurkhan Beg etc., commanded the Maratha naval army.

Other Muslim persons such as Qazi Haider[41] and Madari Mehatar occupied higher and trustworthy posts in his state administration. The Muslims enjoyed equal rights and status in judicial local administration. The majority of the subjects of Shivaji's kingdom also lived in the Maratha territories. But Shivaji never compelled the Muslim people to accept Hinduism as their religion. On the contrary the Muslim subjects in his kingdom was afforded equal treatment. Shivaji acted as a guardian of the Muslims in his territory. Under the rule of Shivaji, the Muslims who acquired equal status with the rest of the population of the Hindus also enjoyed the judicial rights equally.

The Mahazar containing the names of different watandars or officers who possessed right to attend the Hajir Majlis, reveals the Muslims had judicial rights and equal status in declaring judicial verdicts taken by local bodies. In the year, 1657 A.D., the Majlis of mamle Murtazabad was attended by Government officers, Deshaks and Muslim Naiks. It appears that nearly seventy-two members including Watandars of Kasba and village hakadars, attended the Majlis of pargana. Among those members following were Muslim persons who participated in deciding the dispute and served as the witnesses to the Judicial Verdict given on the disputable case of Kulkarni Watan of Mauje Khanapur.[42]

Kazi and Naiks	*Government Servants of Designators*
Kazi Abdul Kadir Hakim	Hasan Shah (Hawaldar)
Haibatkhan	Syed Mahmud Bin Syed
Shaikh Imamkhan	Mir Hokhari
Syed Sikandar (Naikwadiyani)	Malik Abdul Husain
Ali Naik	Khan Hasankhan

In other Mahazar[43] of mauje Ped in mamle Murtazabad, we find following Muslim persons who attended the Majlis by enjoying the status of the members of body and participated in conducting the judicial affairs through the Majlis.

Names of Muslim Members

i) Syed Miyaji (Hawaldar)
ii) Maulana Mahammad Husaini Dabir
iii) Sakhavatkhan Alishan (Mehaldar)

In other document an illustration is cited of the fact that the Muslims were the witnesses to the disputes decided by the Brahmasabha and Rajsabha also. The members attending the meeting of Brahmasabha and Rajsabha for giving the verdict on the dispute of Mokadami included Brahmanas, government officials, Watandars and the Muslims.[44] In another meeting of Rajasabha called for declaring judgement on the dispute of Mokadami of Mauje Pargaon of Poona prant arose between Lumajee and Kondaji, one Muslim Naikwadi namely Itabarkhan[45] was present at the time of conducting the judicial business. The Muslim person was one of the witnesses to the settlement of the dispute and acquired equal status alongwith other Hindu members of the judicial body by accompanying them. Thus the above mentioned evidences make us believe that the Muslims were also allowed to work as the guarantors in judicial cases and were treated most justly by King Shivaji. The cited illustrations reflect not only on Shivaji's faith in Muslim people as king's trustees but also on his sense of justice.

Persian Influence of Judicial Administration

In historical original documents pertaining to the reign of King Shivaji, we find a considerable influence of Muslim system of justice on Maratha king's judicial institution. The Persian influence on Shivaji's administration of justice can be observed in the judicial terms and the court nomenclature. The Persian words such as Majlis, Diwan, Hawaldar, Mokadam, Munsafi,

Hakaljima, Munsifadar, Mahazarnama, Takasimi etc., used in judicial departments of the king were exactly similar to those of the Muslim rule in India. The strong Muslim influence fell on judicial system of Shivaji can obviously be seen from the Persian word like Huzur Hazir Majlis, used for the king's court of justice. In the judicial procedure and in the judgements declared by judicial local bodies, called as "Mahazar" the Persian nomenclature is evident. The Persian element like Sijil was also included in the Mahazar.[46] Regarding Hindu Muslim elements contained in it, Dr. Gune V.T., has rightly pointed out that the Mahazar was an excellent mixture of the Muslim and indigenous institution of local administration.[47] Wahed Husain while emphasising on the influence of Mughal rule remarks that King Shivaji also followed the model of Mughal administrative system. He made a deliberate attempt to give a Hindu colour to his administrative machinery by substituting Sanskrit titles for Persian ones at his court. Most of the names of the departments, records and subordinate officials of the state remained Islamic where they were not indigenous Marathi.[48]

Capital Punishment never Inflicted

When we study the records containing the evidences of forms and methods of punishment it would appear that King Shivaji believed in severe punishments and he very carefully inflicted them too. A careful examination of the documents makes us believe that the capital punishment was not in use under Shivaji's rules. It seems that Shivaji never prescribed the death penalty to the offenders. But the punishment of cutting of the limbs like eyes,[49] hands, legs[50] etc., was commonly prescribed for the serious crimes. King Shivaji also prohibited killing or capturing women, children in the territory of the enemy. Subhasad[51] states that Shivaji followed this rule very strictly. The king never permitted his men to capture children or women during war period. He asked his soldiers to pay respects and protect the enemy's women and the Muslim saints, the religious books found during war time. War prisoners were never punished by Shivaji.

REFERENCES AND FOOTNOTES

1. Manu Samhita, Chapters 8, 9 and also 10
2. Narad, Legal procedure, III, 7, and P. 35
3. Altekar A.S., Caste and Government in Ancient India, P. 247
3a. Ganganath Jha, Manusmriti, The Laws of Manu with the Bhasya of Medhatithi, Vol. III, Part II P. 292
4. MIS, VIII, Letter No. 28
5. CSP, Letter No. 189.
6. Peshwa Diaries XXXI, Letter No. 39
7. Rajwade V.K., MIS, VIII, Letter No. 32
8. Shri Shivdigvijaya (ed.) Dhere R.C., P. 50
9. Ibid, P. 50
9a. Ajna Patra, P. 79
10. AP, Chapter No. 4 P. 87-88
11. Bendre V.S., Kesava Pandit's Dandaniti (1943) P. 16
12. Purandare Daftar, Part III, Deshpande's (Taluka Khedebare) Karina of Shivaji's period P. 134
13. Ibid, Part III, P. 141
14. Gune V.T., JSM, P. 130
15. Peshwa Diaries, XXXI Letter No. 39, also see Chhatrapati Shivaji Maharajanchi Patre, Letter No.177
16. SPSS,III, Letter No. 2778
17. CSP, Letter No. 178
18. SCS 7, Letter No. 41
19. Joshi S.N., Arvachin Maharashtratil Rajya Karbharacha Abhyas, I, P. 208
20. Pagadi Setu Madhavrao, Chhatrapati Shivaji P. 293
21. Jadunath Sarkar, Tarikhe Shivaji, quoted in Pagadi's Op. Cit., P. 292
22. 91 Qalami Bakhar, P. 144
23. Sarkar J.N., Tarikhe Shivaji, quoted in Pagadi's Op. Cit., P. 292
24. 91 Qalami Bakhar, P.144
25. SPSS I, Letter No. 510
26. SPSS I, Letter No. 1830
27. SPSS I, Letter No. 1831

28. Purandare Dafter, III, Letter No. 152, also see SPSS, III, Letter No. 2610
29. Rajwade V.K., MIS, VIII, Letter No. 31
30. SPSS I, Letter Nos. 510
31. Joshi S.N., Arvachin Maharashtratil Rajya Karbharacha Abhyas, Part I, P. 208
32. SCS, I, Letter Nos. 59 and 60
33. SCS, III, Letter No. 427
34. Sampradayik Vividh Vishyak Lekh, 99, quoted in Shejwalkar's Shrishiv Chhatrapati P. 481
35. SCS 7, Letter No. 41
36. Shejwalkar T.S., Srishiv Chhatrapati P. 481
37. Chhatrapti Shivaji Maharajanchi Patre, Letter No. 4
38. SPSS I, Letter No. 696
39. Ibid, I, Letter Nos. 726, 826
40. Shejwalkar T. S., Op. Cit. P. 375
41. Sardesai G.S., NHM, I, P. 208
42. SCS, III, Letter No. 637
43. Ibid, III, Letter No. 638, PP. 221-222
44. Sanada Patre, Prakaran 4, Lekh No. 9, quoted in Gune V.T., Op. Cit. PP 188-189
45. SCS II, Letter No. 98, P. 123
46. Chitnis K. N., Socio-Economic Aspects of Medieval India, P. 223
47. Gune V. T., Op. Cit. P. 139
48. Wahed Husain, Administration of Justice During the Muslim Rule in India, P. 105
49. SCS, II, Letter No. 253
50. SPSS, II, Letter No. 510
51. Sabhasad Bakhar, P. 32

2

Disputes Settled by King Shivaji

During Shivaji's period, we find that king's judicial court at the centre and other local courts in the province were performing the judicial functions. At the centre, Chhatrapati Shivaji, and his Chief Judge and Panditrao decided the suits brought before them. Rajasbha or the Dharma Sabha was noteworthy judicial body helping the king in deciding the cases of disputes. Brahma Sabha was another judicial assembly which also assisted the Chhatrapati Shivaji in declaring judgements on religious matters. The Subha or Pargana majlis also known as Gotasabha, the tarf majlis or Kasba Gotasabha and the village majlis or mauje Gotasabha etc., were the judicial bodies which administered justice in all parts of the Subha or pargana.

We may mention the names of those courts of justice in the tabular form as under.

Courts of Justice (Majlis) during Shivaji's period

Name of the Court	*Presiding Officer*
The Rajsabha or the Huzur Hazir Majlis (Dhamasabha)	Chhatrapati Shivaji or (His Minister or state officials)
The Brahma Sabha	Dharmadhikari
The Subha or Pargana Majlis (Pargana Gotasabha)	Subhedar of the Deshmukh
Kasba Gotasabha or Tarf Majlis	Shete–Mahajan
The village Majlis or village Gotasabha	Mokadam

Chhatrapati Shivaji

Chhatrapati Shivaji, being the head of the Maratha Kingdom, used to decide suits and also hear appeals at his court on Raigad. King Shivaji who observed the practice of administering justice in person sat in the court or heard appeals by remaining present in the Rajsabha or Dharmasabha. Shivaji allowed his men to report to him about their grievances by remaining present in the court. With an aim of administering the justice to his subjects, the king also appointed the Chief Judge (Nyayadhish) and the Panditrao. Many suits brought before the Government officials like Subhedar, the Deshmukh, the Mokadam etc., the heads of the local units, were decided with the help of the Gotasabha.

Nyayadhish and His Qualifications

The supreme authority over all judicial cases was undoubtedly that of King Shivaji. Nyayadhish and Panditrao gave him assistance in deciding those disputes. Shivaji transferred some of the important cases to refer them to a qualified justice who was selected by the king himself. The competent person well learned in Hindu sastras or in the laws was appointed by Shivaji as the Chief Justice of his Kingdom. The Chief Justice and Panditrao of Shivaji's Kingdom were similar to the Pradhan and Pandita of the Sukraniti.[1] Usually, King Shivaji selected his Nyayadhish from among the Brahman community. The Chief Judges of the king possessed the qualities of wisdom, intelligence[2] and cunningness. They were perfectly wise and foresighted men.[3] The Judge appointed by the king was a man of honesty[4] and impartiality and obtained a detailed knowledge of Hindu customs and laws. The Sabhasad Bakhar has described the qualities of the Panditrao or a judge as a Scholar well versed in four Vedas, Shaddarshanas, and also in studies of Yogas.[5] The Chief Justice should have full knowledge of all sciences including the Jyotish Sastra.[6] Shri Shivdigvijay Chronicle seems to have adopted similar attitude regarding the Judge and describes that the Chief Justice should be thorough gentleman, a person of high born family and highly intelligent. He must be well versed in the Dharma Sastras.[7] King Shivaji had a high regard for the Chief Justice and gave him respect is obvious from the fact that in the royal court, the Nyayadhish alongwith king's other ministers was standing with great respect.[8] The king thought his Chief Justice as a trustworhy, faithful, wise, impartial and respectable man. This may be borne out by the evidence that he bestowed the royal award upon him in form of robes of honour.[9] During Shivaji's reign, the office of Chief Justice seems to be hereditary in the family of Niraji Rauji, after whose death, his son, Pralhad Niraji held the post. Apart from his duty of administering the justice to the people in Maratha Kingdom, the Chief Justice had also to accompany the king or to act as a general when the latter undertook the military campaigns against his enemy.

CASES DECIDED BY KING SHIVAJI OR IN HIS PRESENCE

We shall now discuss the cases of disputes brought before King Shivaji and also the judgements given on them by himself or in his presence. When the complaint was lodged to the king or to his officer, the latter summoned the Majlis or referred the cases to the Gotamajlis for the judgement. But on many occasions, King Shivaji decided the cases in the court in person. In the following pages, some notable cases on which the king himself gave the verdicts are cited for understanding his impartial attitude towards justice.

Criminal Cases

Criminal cases like committing adultery and robbery were decided by King Shivaji himself. In 1646 A.D., Babaji Bhikaji Gujar, a mokadam of mauje Ranje committed an act of illicit in the village. The report about his misconduct was sent to the king immediately by the Deshmukh and the Kulkarni of tarf Khedebare. Shivaji issued an order to his officer to bring the mukadam in his presence for trial. After making an investigation of his act, it came to know that the charge kept against the person proved as true. King Shivaji punished him by confiscating his watan and also ordered to cut off his feet and hands. The criminal was sent into the prison till his death.[10] Babaji Bhikaji Gujar was to pay the penalty of three hundred hons to the king who recovered it from Sonaji Banaji Gujar, the relative of the criminal.[11]

Another decision given by Shivaji, which shows a peculiarity of his fearlessness, in inflicting the punishment on the offender was the case of Sakhuji Gaikwad, a brother-in-law of King Shivaji.[12] Sakhuji Gaikwad was a higher officer in the army. When the Maratha troops were marching to Belwadi, Savitribai, the widow of Desai, opposed them. But in a fight that took place between Shivaji's army and the troops of Desai, Savitribai was defeated. She was captured and kept in prison. Sakhuji Gaikwad misbehaved with her and committed a serious crime. Shivaji received a complaint and heard about the wicked deed of Sakhuji Gaikwad. On listening of the news, Shivaji immediately held his trial.

After completing necessary investigation of the evidences in support of the offence, the king declared him criminal and punished him by imprisoning him till his death. The king was not satisfied with this penalty. He issued an order that the offender should be blinded by putting out his eyes.[13] A case of criminal offence decided by King Shivaji was the adultery committed by Rango Trimal Wakada, a village Kulkarni in Taluka Musekhore. The Kulkarni committed rape on a Brahmin widow of that village. The Sardeshmukh and the Deshmukh of the pargana made a complaint against Rango Trimal to King Shivaji who on hearing of the matter ordered that the offender would be imprisoned and be brought before his court. But the offender, out of fear, before the imprisonment fled away by deserting the territory of Shivaji and resorted to Jawali region, that was in the possession of Chandrarao More. But later on the offender died there

King's Judgements on Civil Disputes

Sakho Bhikaji of tarf Khedebare had made a complaint to King Shivaji regarding the dispute of Kulkarni Watan of tarf Khedebare. The plaintiff presented the unknown fact before the king that the Watan was granted and was continued in his family from the time when his grandfather namely Rudraji Narayan enjoyed it. His father was also granted the Watan of the villages of Khede Kasba and Shiwapur. The plaintiff presented a written statement (Karina) to the king in detail about how he was deprived of the claim over the Kulkarni Watan. He added in the statement that Bapujipant who was living in Kasba spoke a lie with queen Jijabai, the mother of the King that the Kulkarni Watan belonged to him only and he requested the mother queen that the same Watan should be transferred to him. Bapujipant also misguided the king by wrongly stating that Bhikaji Rudra committed a theft in Kasba. On hearing the news probably, of the Rajsabha wherein following members were present for taking the decision on the case of Bhikaji Rudra. King Shivaji by presiding over the Rajsabha, summoned other prominent officers such as Ragho Ballal Atre, Sonaji Pant Dabir and Bhanaji Ballal to be present. Other officers of Kasba who attended the majlis (Rajsabha) were as follows :

Bapuji Damodhar (Hawaldar and Majumdar of Peth or Kasba)	Babuji Naik-Deshmukh Bopaji Naik-Deshmukh Kanaji Naik-Deshmukh Bhiwaji Naik-Deshmukh Ramaji Naik-Deshmukh Nagoji Nawadkar (Diwan of Deshmukh)

Thus, with the decision taken in presence of king, the Kulkarni Watan of the Kasba was taken over from Bhikaji and it was conferred on Bapuji. Later on Siwaji Awaji who was a Kulkarni of the village of Nasarapur, also claimed for the half of the said Watan of Khedebare. But Bapuji not only refused his claim over the Watan, but also severely beat him. Hence with an aim of removing the unjustices done by Bapuji on Siwaji Awaji, the father of the plaintiff approached the Deshmukh for administering the justice to him. But the Deshmukh replied that the king by supporting his pratyawadi, has favoured him. The officer had no reason to grumble against the king. The Kulkarni watan would be conferred on him only when the king would decide the matter in his favour. After some days, Bapujipant died and his son Naro Bapuji served King Shivaji and Naro Bhikaji, the brother of plaintiff was the Kulkarni of Sivapur. When Fatekhan the Bijapuri Vassal invaded king's territory, the peace treaty was made with him by ceding him the fort of Kondhana and province of Sirwal Khedebare. Then King Shivaji arrived at Poona and Abaji Mahadev became his diwan. At that time, Naro Bapoji, the father of plaintiff, accompanied by Mahadeo Bhat came to Poona and appeared before king and requested him that Naro Bapoji was financially weak and by paying five hons to the Diwan, Naropant was granted the Kulkarni Watan. Then political discontent caused by

Bapuji, the diwan of Adilshah, also disturbed and plundered the peth. Hence Shivaji came to the peth to protect it and collected one hundred takas as mohim patti. But Naro Bapuji made a complaint to the king against his brother, Naro Bhikaji, that the latter did not look after the peth for more than ten or twelve months. Naro Bhikaji was also blamed for committing of the theft for which he was punished by the king by depriving him from the right of Watan and conferring it on Naro Bapuji. Thus, the Kulkarni Watan was taken from the grand father of the plaintiff and was transferred to another person. Therefore, the plaintiff again approached the king for reconsideration of the case. He requested King Shivaji to issue an order to the Deshmukh for deciding the dispute. The king granted his request and asked Mukund Dhondadev Atre, the hawaldar, Babaji Janardhan the Majumdar, and also the Deshmukh to decide the dispute by holding the meeting of the majlis at another place. But Bapuji Chimanaji refused to approach the Deshmukh of some other place for hearing the judgement.

The Deshmukh of the pargana reported to King Shivaji on Raigad that Chimanaji Bapuji was not willing to go to other majlis for the correct justice. After receiving the report from the Deshmukh, Shivaji issued an instruction to Chimanaji that he had forcefully taken the Kulkarni Watan from Sakho Bhikaji. Therefore, he was advised by Shivaji to hand over the said Watan to Sakho Bhikaji. The Government officer Deshmukh sent the King's advice to Chimanaji to give his consent for the transfer of the place of majlis. Thereupon, Chimanaji agreed to change the place of justice and finally he agreed to obey the decision given by Chaudoji Ballal. Therefore, the plaintiff again appeared before the king at Raigad and reported the matter to him in detail. Then, as per the order of the king, the case was referred to Chawadaji of Peth Siwapur for the correct decision. But Chimanaji who brought Monaji Naik as his witness, gave four maunds of grain to him for the untruth, he should speak that Bapuji had made a demand to his right over Kulkarni Watan of Kasba from Rudraji Narayan. But the latter denied his right over the Watan. Then, after some days, the plaintiff approached Rajashri Shivaji and appealed him to decide the case in his favour. King Shivaji called a meeting of Majlis which was attended by Peshwa, Babaji Naik, Raghunath Pant Korade, Trimbak Pant Dabir, and Chaudoji Ballal. He requested the members of the majlis that his Watan had been confiscated by force. He appealed them that the Watan would be restored to him. King Shivaji thought over this dispute and replied that Sakho Bhikaji spoke the truth that could be acceptable to dharma. But Chimanaji did unjustice on Sakhoji by using his prestige and status. He also did not approach to other place for the decision. Therefore, the king thought that Chimanaji seemed to him to be proved as wrong and his claim over the Watan would be rejected on such ground. Meanwhile, Chimanaji got the mahzar of the dispute regarding the Watan. He got newly written but a forged mahzar on which the Deshmukh Shete, Mahajan had attested their signs of designation. The newly prepared mahzar showed that Sakho Bhikaji's claim over the Watan was wrong and hence his claim was declared to be set aside. Chimanaji said to have succeeded in the case because of the forged document. But in fact the decision of Sakho Bhikaji's case was not declared by the king or the Majlis because Shivaji had launched a campaign against Bardesh[15] and was absent from home for some days. The decision on Watan dispute thus remained unsettled till Shivaji's life. Another case that was decided by the king himself with the consultation of Gota, was the dispute regarding the Kulkarni Watan of tarf Pen between Abaji Kito and Sarango Sahdev. The Kulkarni Watan of tarf Pen had been conferred upon Ambaji Kito and his brother Pantaji Kito. The latter enjoyed the right on half of the Watan and Sarango Sahdev enjoyed the right on one-third part of the Watan. After the death of Pantaji Kito, Sarango Sahdev though looked after the Watan enjoyed only one-third part of the total income of the

Watan. Therefore, he appeared before King Shivaji and applied for an equal share in the Kulkarni Watan. The plaintiff demanded that the Watan should be divided equally between two partners. He appealed to King Shivaji that the justice should be given to him. He replied to the king that he (Plaintiff) would be satisfied if the decision on the Watan would be given by the king or by the Gota. The king called the Gota of the village for dispensing the justice to Sarango Sahdev. Th Gota through majlis decided that the Watan would be equally divided between Sarango Sahdev and Ambaji Kito. As per its verdict, Sarango Sahdev was allowed to enjoy the half of his Watan as long as he was alive. After his death, his nephew namely Mahadev was allowed to enjoy the half of the Watan.[16] Thus, a letter of decision regarding the Settlement of Kulkarni Watan between Sarango Sahdev and Ambaji Kito of Pen was prepared by Gota. The Deshakas were the witnesses to the title deed of Watan settlement that was finally approved by King Shivaji. The dispute of Mirasi arose between Satowa Gurav and Ragh Darna Gurav, the worshipper of goddess Srishivan at Jejuri was decided by King's mother Jijabai.[17] The details of the decision are not available in the document. But it is clearly mentioned in the record that the Judgement on Mirasi dispute was declared by Jijamata and it was approved by King Shivaji too. Another dispute of Deshmukhi Watan of Mosekhore arose in 1649–50 A.D., between Baji Yashwantrao and Balaji Yashwantrao. Balalji was conducting the Deshmukhi Watan when Baji Yashwantrao was in service of King Shivaji. By making quarrel, Balaji Yashwantrao forcibly took the charge of the Watan from Baji. Hence Baji appeared before the King and made a complaint against Balajirao to Shivaji.

The Statements of the Plaintiff were heard by King Shivaji himself who pronounced the judgement on the case of disputed Watan. The King examined the evidences involving the suit and declared the rights of Baji Yashwantrao over the Deshmukhi watan to be true. But later on, he along with Kavaji was sent to undertake the military expedition of Belsare. Hence, the Watan of the tarf was granted in the name of Kavaji. In that expedition Baji was killed. Therefore, King Shivaji granted the Deshmukhi watan to Krishnaji Yashwantrao. He was named as Sawai Baji who was authorised to look after the administration of the Watan of tarf Mosekhore.[18] A decision dated 26th November, 1655 A.D., of a dispute between Sabaji Pasalkar and Ramaji, Nagoji, Babaji and Dhanaji Balaji etc., about Deshmukhi watan of Mosekhore pargana was given by King Shivaji as stated below. Four brothers lodged a complaint to King Shivaji by remaining present in his court about the Deshmukhi watan that was enjoyed by Dharmaji Balaji. The king called the meeting of the Huzur Hazir Majlis. In deciding the case, the Gota of that place was also consulted. The cause of dispute of the Deshmukhi watan was explained in the following way. The Watan was conferred upon the ancestor of those brothers since the long time. Thereafter, Dharmaji Balaji and others were enjoying the right over the Deshmukhi watan. Their elder brother had no heir. Therefore, after his death, the King made an enquiry as to in whose name the watan of Deshmukh be continued. On the request of Sabaji Yashwantrao who was not elder than Baji, the watan was transferred to his account. In fact, Tulaji Farjand and others were the elder brothers of Sabaji. Though the latter claimed for the elderness wrongly, the watan along with the designation and rights, was transferred to his name. Moreover, Sabaji had also failed in performing the duties of a Deshmukh. The rayat in pargana also became disappointed with his work because the behaviour of the Deshmukh with the people was very stern and hard. Therefore, the rayat on the contrary was pleased with the son of Tulaji Sabaji who was the eldest among them. The plaintiffs made the request to the King that in place of Sabaji Krishnaji, he (son of Tulaji) should be granted the Deshmukhi watan with all rights, perquisites and designation. They further requested the King that just as all other brothers were enjoying the right over the Watan, Sabaji would be regarded as one of the younger partners of the watan and the Deshmukhi watan should be transferred to Tulaji only. After hearing the detailed account of the eligible and capable person's claim for the Deshmukhi watan, Shivaji who was assured, granted the watan to the same person in whose favour other brothers had made the demand to the King.[19] King Shivaji dispensed justice personally in case of the dispute[20] over the Deshmukhi watan of Gunjanmawal arose in 1657 A.D., among Habaji Babaji Silambkar, Bapuji Kanhoji Silambkar and Balaji Rudraji Silambkar. The Hazir Majlasi met at Poona was presided over by Rajshri Chhatrapati Shivaji and was attended by prominent members such as Samraj Nilkanth Peshwa, Sonaji Dabir, Balaji Naik Punde, Manakoji Dahatonde, Sarnobat Nurbeg, Sarnobat Abaji, Mahadev Hejib Vasudev Balkrishna Majumdar, Mahadaji Shamraj Surnis, Balaji Hari, Raghunath Ballal Sarsabnis, Shamraj Sabnis the Deshmukh of Velhavandkhore, the mokadams of Bhowargaon, Sonde Mohari Budruk, Adauli, Pakhadi, Tale, Kodalwadi Borale and Ambone and the Deshaks and the Kulkarni of Gunjanmawal etc. Before twenty years, the same dispute was decided by Dadaji Kondadev, the Subhedar by summoning the Gotasabha.[21] But the litigants were dissatisfied with that decision. Therefore, again in 1657 A.D. the quarrel began among them. King Shivaji gave decision by equally dividing the watan and its seniority rights among Shivaji, Habaji and Bapuji. The King dispensed justice to Balaji by affording him the equal status and prestige which was enjoyed earlier by Habaji and Bapuji.[22] A dispute regarding the boundary between two villages of Kalbauli in Pannumaul pargana and Mauje Rawade of Paudkhore taluka arose in 1658 A.D. King Shivaji had already informed the Deshadhikari and other officers of prant Waramawal about the boundary dispute between those villages. One of the inhabitants of the village namely Arjoji Dhamala argued that he would be able to determine the true boundary of the village by performing an ordeal. But the day on which the ordeal was to be performed by the person in presence of all the Deshakas, Arjoji Dhamala remained absent and could not prove as successful. The King got the report about the non-performance of an ordeal by Arjoji Dhamala when the former was busy with some other important political matters for which Shivaji had to leave the territory of swaraj and went to the province of alien rule. Therefore, the decision on the boundary dispute between those villages was postponed and the dispute remained unsettled. But till then, the villagers were instructed by the State officers to regard the kasland lying in between the two villages as their boundary.[23] A decision on 5th January, 1669 A.D. on a dispute of Kulkarni watan of mauje Sonori of Poona pargana between Govinda Vishwanath and Ramaji Krishna of Kasba Saswad, containing in the mahzar, is not complete. The village Gota gave its verdict on this suit by preparing a mahzar which declared Ramaji Krishna Gavkhanderau's rightful claim to the Kulkarni Watan of mauje Sonori. But the complainant, Govind Panashi was not satisfied with the justice dispensed by the local judicial body. Therefore, he (the complainant) personally brought the complaint before King Shivaji in the court and made him a request to give him the justice. For dispensing the impartial justice, the proper judicial authority asked the plaintiff and defendant to submit their statements in detail.[24]

As the record is incomplete, the information regarding King's further decision on that case is not available to us. A case of disputed Kulkarni watan of Timaji Khanderao of mauje Kolhale of Supe pargana presented before King in court by the plaintiff himself is worth noticing. The Kulkarni watan of said mauje was purchased for twenty hons by Timaji Khanderau from Rakhamaji and Antaji Unda Pandarkar during famine period. But Visaji and Rakhamaji, the sons of Unda went to Supe and offered bribe to the hawaldar who imprisoned Timaji Khanderao. The hawaldar took away forcibly from him the mahzar of

Watan prepared by the Gota. The complainant later on went to Karnataka to meet King Shahaji and reported him everything about what had happened. On hearing the case, King Shahaji issued an order to the Deshmukh of the pargana to call the meeting of the Gota for taking the decision about the case of Timaji Khanderao. Thereafter, the plaintiff arrived at Jejuri where he learnt that King Shivaji ordered to capture Sambhaji Mohite, the hawaldar of Supe. Therefore, he appeared before King Shivaji and lodged a complaint against Visaji and Ramaji Unda Pandarkar. He requested the King that the justice should be administered to him. On hearing the complaint the King called upon the plaintiff and also the defendants to remain present in the court. King Shivaji ordered the Deshmukh and Deshkulkarni of Pune pargana to call the meeting of the Gotasabha to give the verdict on this suit. The Gotsabha convened as per the instructions of King Shivaji and presided over by the Deshmukh of the pargana, was attended by following members, who were invited there.

Deshmukh of Poona Pargana	*Deshkulkarni of Poona Pargana*
Maloji Narsingrau Sitole	Vitthal Mordeu
Vithoji Naik Sitole	Babaji Rama

Pargana Supe

Shamrajkate Deshmukh	Babadebhat Joshi
Chandaguda Khaira	Chandrabhat Joshi
Herodara Mokadam	*Deshkulkarni*
Mahajan and Shete Kasba Supe	Vitthal Mahadu Trimbak Gomdeu Timaji Malhar Malhar Babaji Kulkarni Sauji and Malaji Khomana Mokadam Mauje Kolhale

After investigating into the statements of both the parties, it was found that Sambhaji Mohite, an officer of Supe prant involved in bribery by accepting seventy-five hons for conferring the watan on Pandarkar brothers Sambhaji Mohite forcefully persuaded Timaji to give over that Kularni watan to Pandarkar. But the officer brought a lot of pressure on Timaji by beating him or sending him into the prison, to give his consent for the sale of the Kulkarni Watan to Pandarkar for twenty hons. King Shivaji severely condemned the misconduct of the officer of the plaintiff made by him. Shivaji with the help of Gotasabha gave the decision that the Kulkarni watan would be restored to Timaji Khanderau. The amount of bribery was to be refunded by the officer to Pandarkar in form of a horse which belonged to Sambhaji Mohite. Shivaji took the action not only against the Government officer, but also against the persons who offered the bribe to the Hawaldar. Thus, the Mahzar which declared the decision of the King with the help of Gota, was prepared and signed by the following members,[25] who acted as the witnesses to the above decision.

Witnesses

Rangoji Mokadam Nimbalkar mauje Wadga (Poona)	Naikwadi Pargana Supe
Madaji Mokadam mauje Jalga	Itbarkhan
Haraji Malwadkar	Abhangarau
Lukhoji Khomana (Mokadam)	Ravirau
Babaji Tanaji	Babaji More
Mahipati Narsoji	Yeshwantrao Jadhav Mokadam
Parsoji Raghoji	Nagoji Potter

Yekoji Tanhaji	Yamaji Gurav
Naroji Rambhaji	Naik Mahar
Malaji Godaji	Dharoji Potadar
Balutas	*Balutas of Supa*
Bhika Carpenter	Kankoji and Lakhamoji Nhavi
Yelha Mahar	Nagoji and Yema
Bahira Cobbler	Mehatari Cobbler Khand Naik Mahar

Another case was decided by King Shahaji, the father of Shivaji, in April 1651 A.D. The case was about the dispute on the Deshmukhi watan between Samaraj and Sambhaji Kate resided in the pargana. Sambhaji Kate remained present at King's court and requested him that the Deshmukhi should be equally divided between Samraj Kate and Sambhaji Kate. After hearing the complaint, the King examined his statements with the help of Deshak of mahal and was pleased to issue an order to the Deshmukh of the pargana declaring the verdict in favour of the plaintiff. The meeting of the Deshak[26] was attended by the eminent persons such as Hirjoji Walhoji Sambhaji Atole, Hatkararau, Sawaji and Malaji Khanaji and Malaji Khomane etc., who decided the case as guided by the King. King Shivaji decided the dispute on the Shetewatan of the Peth between Gopalsheth Seti and Jauseti Kadatseti Mahajan in the year 1665 A.D. Jauseti Mahajan had made a complaint to the King that after the death of Mawaseti the Shetewatan was conferred upon him. Sultan Malik Ambar had also issued the Sanad granting him the Shetewatan of the peth. But later on, the name of another person namely Mawaseti. The complainant told the King that this was an act of unjustice. He further narrated that when he appeared before Netaji Palkar (Subhedar, and executive officer) for the justice, the latter gave the same decision as stated above. King Shivaji who investigated the necessary documents with the help of Gotasabha, decided that the Shetewatan should be continued in the family of Gopalsheth Seti.[27] The King was pleased to declare that Gopal Seti and his sons were to act as shete of the peth by enjoying all the rights of the watan. A peculiar case of dispute between three brothers namely Abaji Tawaji, Balaji Tawaji, and Dadaji, on the distribution of father's wealth or money was settled by King Shivaji with the help of his officer. The case shows that the suits of disputed wealth or property were also brought before the King for the decision. Balaji Tanaji Deshmukh and Deshkulkarni of mamale Cheul presented his case personally before King's court by saying that previously three brothers were staying together in a joint family and possessed the common rights over their father's wealth. Then they were separated from each other. At the time of the separation it was decided in presence of some respected men in society that every one of them should have equal share in their father's wealth or money. But after some days, Apaji and Dadaji refused to give his share to Balaji Tawaji from their father's money. Thus, the brothers of the plaintiff committted an act of unjustice. Therefore, Balaji made a request to King Shivaji to give him justice in this regard. On hearing the statements of Balaji, the King gave an order to Ramaji Mahadu Prabhu, the hawaldar of mamle Cheul, to dispense justice to Balaji. The King asked the hawaldar to abstain the brothers of the complainant from excluding him from his right over father's property.[28] The officer was further instructed by the King to issue them a letter of warning that if they did so, they woud have to face serious consequences.

A dispute regarding the Deshmukhi watan[29] arose between Sarjerao, Siwaji, Chandaji and Rayaji and Sambhaji Jedhe of tarf Rohidkhore in 1668–69 A.D. All those brothers except Sarjerao came before King Shivaji and made him a request to dispense justice to them regarding the rights over the watan among all those brothers. King Shivaji heard their complaints regarding every one's rights over the Deshmukhi watan. The Jedhe brothers except Sarjerao had to await for the decision for a period of a month. The eldest brother Sarjerao did not appear before the King. So King Shivaji issued an order to Sarjerao to remain present before the King. But the latter failed to come up to the King. Therefore, the King came to know that Sarjerao was not willing to distribute the rights over the watan among his brothers. He decided the case according to the rules of Hindu Dharmasastras and granted the rights of watan in the name of Jedhe brothers. The King also issued them the document of the verdict regarding the rights of an individual over the Deshmukhi watan of tarf Rohidkhore. King Shivaji declared the verdict on the dispute of the Upadhya Watan of Kasba Dehaya of taluka Devale arose between Trimalbhat, Janardhanbhat, Rudrabhat, Vishwanathbhat in the month of March 1676. Atolye Upadhya remained present in King's court and lodged a complaint before him by asserting that the Upadhya watan of eight villages was a hereditary watan conferred upon his forefathers and since then, it had been continued in his family. But, meanwhile, Govindbhat who brought interruption in his enjoyment and the right of watan, made it a disputed thing by challenging the claim of the plaintiff over the Watan.[30] The King, on hearing the statements of the complainant called a meeting of the Deshak of the taluka and asked them to make an enquiry about the claim of Atolye over the Upadhya watan. In an investigation, the claim of Govindbhat proved to wrong. Therefore, the King with the help of the Deshak, gave decision by issuing an order to Ramaji Anant the Subhedar of Prabhavali to declare that the hereditary watan had been continued in the name of Atolye. The King further instructed the Subhedar to issue the strict warning to Govindbhat for not giving him (plaintiff) trouble thereafter. If he failed in acting so, the officer was ordered to give the punishment to Govindbhat.

The study of the civil and criminal cases tried by King Shivaji and the judgements pronounced by him reveal that the Maratha King's judicial system was undoubtedly based upon the principle of impartiality and justice as well as on the consideration of equality of all men before the law and justice.

King's Hearing of an Appeal

The case was taken against the judgement of lower courts like the village Majlis, pargana Majlis, and Subha Majlis and finally it came up to the King's court. In fact the person involved in the dispute if dissatisfied with the decision given by earlier court, could possess right to take his case direct to the ruler. He would make an appeal to the King against the judgement declared by the Subhedar also. For instance, a disputed case of Deshmukhi watan of Gunjanmawal was tried by Dadaji Kondadev, the Subhedar of fort Kondana on 26th of January, 1638 A.D. But the persons such as Habaji, Bapuji and Balaji etc., involved in the dispute, were dissatisfied with the earlier decision and appealed to King Shivaji who examined the case and reviewed it carefully. On investigating into the dispute, Shivaji found the decision of the Subhedar to be false. He declared that the seniority rights were to be enjoyed not only by Habaji himself but also to be enjoyed by the son of Rudraji.[31] The King who acted as a court of appeal equally divided the seniority rights over the Deshmukhi watan of pargana Gunjanmawal between two persons who were senior than other complainants.

Interruption in King's Routine of Judicial Work

The routine work of pronouncing the judgements by King Shivaji was occasionally interrupted during the course of his military expeditions which he undertook in other's territory. The contemporary records speak how the criminal cases or the most important civil cases were to be dealt with by Shivaji himself. An excellent example of boundary dispute of the villages of Kalbauli in Paunmawal pargana and mauje Rawade can be well illustrated here when Shivaji heard that Arjoji Dhamala[32] did not perform an ordeal, he sent an order to his officer of the pargana to postpone the decision regarding the boundary dispute as the King was busy in undertaking an expedition in other territory. After returning from the military invasion the King wanted to investigate the complicated case and to decide it by consulting all the evidences. Till then he asked his officer to issue an order to the villages to regard the Kasland as the boundary between two villages.

REFERENCES AND FOOTNOTES

1. Lallahji Gopal, Sukraniti, a nineteenth Century Text, P. 40
2. Sabhasad Bakhar, P. 104
3. Ibid, P. 70
4. Ibid, P. 107
5. Ibid, P. 100
6. Ibid
7. Dhere R.C., Shri Shivdigvijaya, PP. 50–51
8. Ibid, P. 298
9. Ibid, PP. 301–302
10. SPSS I, Letter No. 627
11. Marathi Daftar Rumal No. 3, Lekh No. 11
12. Pagari's Chhatrapati Shivaji, P. 293
13. 91 Qalami Bakhar, P. 144
14. MIS, XIV, Letter No. 270
15. Shivkalin Karina of Deshpande (Tal Khedebare), Purandare Daftar, Part III, PP. 130–144
16. Khobrekar, Records of the Shivaji period, Letter No. 16, PP. 22–24
17. SCS, II, Letter No. 139
18. SPSS, III, Letter No. 2559
19. SPSS, I, Letter No. 700
20. MIS, XVII, Letter No. 10
21. MIS, XVII, Letter No. 7
22. Gune V.T., JSM, P. 183
23. CSP, Letter No. 69
24. Watan Patre, P. 13, also see Chhatrapati Shivaji Maharajanchi Patre, Letter No. 102
25. SCS, 7, letter No. 44
26. Ibid 7, Letter No. 38

27. MIS, 17, Letter No. 57,
28. SCS, 10, Letter No. 11
29. SPSS, III, Letter Nos. 2712 and 2713
30. SPSS, II, Letter No. 1829
31. SPSS, I, Letter No. 722
32. CSP, Letter No. 69

3

Rajsabha and Brahmasabha

HUZUR HAZIR MAJLIS (RAJSABHA OR DHARMASABHA)

This central judicial body consisted of the King, his Chief Judge and the Panditrao, a minister for religion and also the state officials. The King who was the supreme authority of justice, used to dispense justice with the help of his ministers mentioned above. A large number of cases decided by King Shivaji himself reveal that he acted as a judge and tried different cases of dispute, independently or with the consultation of the Chief Justice or the Panditrao. King Shivaji and his Rajsabha also was regarded as the court of appeal against the justice administered by the local courts. Rajmandal also called as Rajmudra, consisting of the King, his ministers and the officers of the higher ranks acted as King's court of law. The members of the Rajmandal used to give the advice to Chhatrapati Shivaji when he dispensed the justice. The members of the Rajsabha had to put their signatures on the royal decisions or the orders issued by the King to the subhedars, the hawaldars in the Subha[1] or pargana.

It is worth noting here to explain the nature of composition and functions of Rajsabha and it can be best understood from citing some concrete instances. In the following list, the names of notable majalasis and their seals, attending the Rajsabha for deciding the dispute regarding the sale of watan of mauje Kudal, are given. On this occasion King Shivaji was present in person and seems to have tried the suit that came before the Hazir Majlis.[2]

Mahzar *King Shivaji*

Prant Kudal, Shak 1586, Shrawan Shuddha Dashmi Friday

Chandkhan	Sikarkhan designator Kudal (Persian seal)	Sabajibin Rayaji Tukarau, Kanoje–Bin Bhan (Persian seal) Pandit
Aba Seti Bin	Nakhoji Bin	Vithoji Kode
Har Seti (Tagaoi)	Tukaji Desai (Uzarde)	Deshmukh (Khedebare)
Visaji Mabhleshwar Deshkulkarni	Abaji Babaji	Gangaji Patel Nadgauda
Ganseti and Bakseti	Padaji	Mokadam Tanhaji Chaugula
Shete Mahajan (Tagadi)	Joshi	(Seal–plough)
Bahiroji (Sissor)		Babaji Patel (plough)
Vaghoji Salwi and Bakoji Salwi (potter) seal wheel Jauji Bhadaji		Bapuji Awasara (Sissor) Rayaji Bin Bhanaji and Khad Bin Bhiu (cobbler)

The list in Mahzar[3] gives the names of officers like Desai, Deshkulkarni, Mokadam, Chaugula, Shete–Mahajan and balutas in the village who were the witnesses to the decision taken by Hazir Majlis of prant Kudal on the dispute of sale of Watan between Suryaji Tubaji Naik Deshmukh and Bapuji Ratnoji Naik Deshmukh of the mentioned Subha. The Mahzar also bears the name and seal of King Shivaji in whose presence the majlis was summoned. The contents of Mahzar shows that the members of Sabha gave their approval to the sale-deed of fifteen bighas of land by Bapuji Naik Deshmukh to Tubaji Naik Deshmukh. Sometimes, the Rajsabha dispensing justice on the dispute of Mokadam's watan, was attended by subhedar, Brahman experts (Mimanshak), Majumdar, Deshmukh, Deshkulkarni, Shete in the pargana. Thus, the Rajsabha[4] summoned at par near Jawali in month of September 1663, was presided over by the Subhedar Makaji Anandrau who was accompanied by other prominent members, and the watandars such as Deshkulkarni, Deshmukh, Shete of Morgir, Patan, Indapur, Wai, Sangal, Satara parganas of Subha Jawali which came under the jurisdiction of Sarnobat Netaji Palkar. King's officer of the highest rank in Subha and other prominent members who attended the Hazir Majlasi Rajsabha were as given below :

Subhedar Makaji Anandrau	Raje Mahadik Raje Palkar Deshkulkarni (Khedebare)

King Shivaji was the supreme authority of judiciary of the Maratha State. The dispute of Deshmukhi watan of Gunjanmawal between three brothers Habaji Haibat Rau, Silambkar, Bapuji Haibat Rau and Balaji Rudraji Naik etc., was once decided by Dadaji Kondadev. But Habaji Babaji was not satisfied with the judgement given by Dadaji Kondadev and the dispute continued thereafter too. Hence the case was referred to the Hazir Majlis called at Poona for reconsideration. The meeting of Hazir Majlis[5] was presided over by King Shivaji on 21 March, 1657 A.D. for settling of the dispute over Deshmukhi watan between Habaji Silambkar and Bapuji Silambkar. Other permanent members who also attended the Hazir Majlis at Poona, and then present at the meeting were as given below:

Rajshri Shivaji Raje:	The highest judicial authority
Kazi Abdul Kazi Mohammud (Seal)	*Prominent Members*
Prominent Members	Vasudev Balkrishna Majumdar
Shamraj Nilkanth Peshwe (Seal Shrishiva)	Mahadaji Samraj Surnis
Sonaji Dabir	Balaji Hari Majalasi
Balaji Naik Punde Majalasi	Raghunath Ballal
Mankoji Dahatonde Sarnobat (seal)	Sarsabnvis
Nurbeg Sarnobat (seal)	Samraj Sabnis
Abaji Mahadev Hejib (seal)	

The remaining members who were also present on this occasion were clerks, Majumdars of parganas like Haveli, Shirval, Khedebare, Paud, Mosekhore, Kadankhore etc. The Deshmukhs, the Deshaks of talaka Gunjanmawal and the mokadams of the villages such as Bhowargaon, Sonde, Mohari, Pakhadi, Kodalwadi, Borale, etc., also attended the Hazir Majalis. Huzur Hazir Majalis that was summoned by King Shivaji himself for giving verdict on the dispute and Nagoji Kalabhar in the temple of Shri Dev (goddess Khandoba) at Pali in February 1675, constituted of the following prominent men of State officials and the watandars of the villages. The King's officers and other members who attended the meeting of Huzur Hazir Majalis were as follows[6] :

Chhatrapati Shivaji : The supreme judicial authority

Rajmudra (King's Officials)

Haraji Raje Mahadik (Seal)	Niraji Rauji
Raghunath Narayan	Naro Nilkanth Majumdar
Moro Trimal Peshwe (seal)	Shamaji Naik Punde
Dattaji Trimal Wakenis	Anand Rau
Nagoji Gujar	Khandoji Wagh
Dadaji Kakade	Jaitaji Kattar, Somaji Naik
Santaji Jagtap	
Krishnaji Naik	

Other persons attending the majlis were the Majumdar, Hawaldar, clerks, Deshaks, Mokadams of Mahals, and Desai's Patels, Kulkarnis, Deshmukhs, Shete-Mahajans etc., from the parganas of Karhad, Wai. The balutas then present at that time, were goldsmith, oilman, coppersmith, weaver, momin, cobbler, carpenter, potter, and mahzar of the villages. The compoition and nature of subha Rajmandal will obviously be revealed from citing the following contents in the mahzarnama of the Hazir Majlis[7] of Subha of Cheul. This Rajmandal which served as the court of law consisted of prominent officers and members and was headed by the highest authority of the Subha. This dispute regarding the sale-deed of Wadi arose between Suryaji Prabhu and Balaji Shamaji Niraji Jiwaji etc., was decided with the attestation of the witnesses who were present at the time of dispensing the verdict taken by the Rajmandal consisted of following officers, Watandars and leading persons in the parganas.

Rajmandal

Antaji Sivarao	Yeshwantrao Anant (Subhedar)
Yesaji Darekar (Subhedar)	Ganoram Majumdar
Bahiraji Pawar (Subhedar)	Rayaji Satak (Prabhu) (Hawaldar)
Dattaji Vitthal Prabhu	Trimbak Shripat (Subhedar)
Antaji Bhaskar (Majumdar)	Krishnaji Chavhan (Subhedar)
Nagoji Waghmare (Hawaldar)	

Deshmukh	*Mahaj or Naik*	
Bhikaji Yesaji	Pilajee Prabhu	Tanhajirau
Shelke Desai	Krishnaji Prabhu	Majumdar
Govaroji Chaudhary	Baba Joshi Rangoba Naik	Jamaji Appaji Desai Deshkularnis of mamle Cheul

Rajmandal[8] at prant level consisting of Deshak and other prominent men in Mahals was attended and headed by Dattaji Trimal. He issued an instruction to the members of Prant Rajmandal to collect necessary articles from each mahal and send them at Chaphal for celebrating the mahanavami festival there. They were further asked to celebrate such festivals in prant. The special feature of the Dharmasabha was that it was composed not only of the members of Rajmandal but also constituted of Government officials known as Rajmudra and the members of the Gotasabha.[9] The Mahazar prepared by the Hazir Majlasi of Supe pargana was known as mahzar of Belsariya. It was the jayapatra (record of decision) regarding the dispute on the rights of mirasi. On an examination of this mahzar, one finds that there arose a dispute between Naraba Belsara[10] and Sonbhat Khada over the rights of Jotishi and Kulkarni Watan of the mirasi rights over nine villages of Supe pargana in 1631 A.D. It appears that by performing an ordeal, Narayan Belsara proved to be legal claimant over the mirasi and Khade proved to be wrong. The plaintiff had performed the ordeal at the place called Amriteshwar. Nag Joshi Belsara received a letter of judgement from that place and with that Jayapatra he arrived at Thane in pargana Supe. There, after hearing and examining the documents, the members of the majlis of Supe pargana prepared the mahzar. Following were the members who attended the majlis and also affixed their designations and handed over it to Belsara party in whose favour the decision was given.

Members of Hazir Majlisi of Pargana

Rayarau Hawaldar	Tuko Nagnath Majumdar
Khabhai Bedlami Sarnobat	Sakho Vitthal Sabnis
Govind Yesaji Chitnis, Clerk	Ramaji Anant
Thanedar Krishnaji Toras Majumdar	Hasham Vyankatrau
Mohammad Ali Khurd Naikwadi	Trimalrau Anantrau Ramrau

Thane Mamle

Trimalrau Tukoji	Trimalrau Bapuji
Balbatrau	Tanhoji
Narsingrau	Yashwantrao Banaji

Deshak

Gosaseti	Daulat Ramaji Mokadam
Dadseti	Amajo Govind Kulkarni

Mokadams

Yesaji Santaji	Village Belsar
Balaji Mehatari	Village Pargaon
Kadat Setiya	Village Pimpari
Santaji Bhavaji	Paragaon
Kanhoji Radoba	Pimpari
Babaji Saloji	Pimpale, Pandare

Desai - Deshkulkarni

Babaji Kale Desai	Mahado Lakhamdeu Deshkulkarni
Babaji Hiroji Mahajan Shete	Manji Desai
Nagbhat Joshi	Tukseti Setiya Sitoji Mahajan
Sonaji and Janoji	Dashamseti Godseti Mehari (Painter)

Though Belsariya possessed the mahzar the mokadam of Sakurde could not execute the decision. Therefore, the plaintiff Naroba Belsara approached to Salabatkhan and made a complaint to him against inactiveness of the mokadam of Sakurde. But meanwhile Khade went to the Siddhi Ambar Bagdad, the hawaldar of said mamle and told him that Belsara was proved as false by performing the ordeal. He requested the officer to call the officer, Belsara before him for deciding the case. The officer called both the parties to give them advice in deciding the matter to refer the case to the Hazir Majlis of Saswad. Then Belsara having taken that patra (which contained the details of ordeal performed by Belsara and decision of the Gotasabha) with him, went to Saswad. From the statements presented before the majlis of Saswad by Belsara, it is evident that Narayan Somaji Khade was the plaintiff and Narayan Belsara was the defendant. Belsara and Khade gave the thalpatra and other documents to the officer of Saswad pargana. Some of the persons who were present at the time of performing the ordeal, were remained present at Saswad. The majlis (Dharmasabha) summoned by Raul and attended by other members consisted of the Rajmudra (Government officials) as given under:

Rajmudra (State Officials)

Rajshri Rayaji Datto Hawaldar (Saswad)	Siwaji Gaikwad

Mahajan and Mahaprusnik (Expert Men in Law)

Baji and Tauji Deshmukh	Honaji and Hiroji
Sabaji Trimal Deshkulkarni	Mokadam Saswad
Sant Seti and Tuka Seti Setiya	Sitaji Mahajan
Sitaji Mahjan	Somaji Teli
Bapuji Chaugula	Seti Rangra Naras Seti

Tamali Mehatare (mokadam mauje Jejuri)

Vitha Seti Sonar

Madaji Malwadkar Tamboli

Malseti Mahajan

Bhikaji Khomane

Baloji Makadam

Somaji Khade gave the reply to the members of the majlis by saying that his father was enjoying the right of mirasi much earlier than that of Belsara's father. Then the majlis asked the plaintiff whether he possessed some papers showing the claim of his father over the watan. Upon this, the plaintiff replied that the documents relating to the vritti were kept in his house at Jejuri. But those papers were taken away at by Belsara. To this, Belsara gave answer that the papers destroyed in the work of digging of the wall of his house, were not related to the watan, but they were pertained to the Government's pattis. After then, on the request made by Nag Joshi, the grand father of the defendant, the dispute was taken to Amriteshwar Mahisala in Konkan for giving the judgement. Alongwith necessary documents the claimants went to other new place. The sabha nayaka of that place examined the statements of both parties and asked Nag Joshi to perform the ordeal. Nag Joshi who succeeded completely in performing the ordeal got the jayapatra from the local sabha of that place. The jayapatra contained the decision declaring to restore mirasi right to Nag Joshi who later on left the village for Kashi. Narayan Belsara, the father of defendant made a demand for the right of mirasi towards the father of Khade who was then enjoying the right over the watan. But the latter denied former's claim over the vritti. Therefore, Khade appeared before Azamkhan, the hawaldar of Saswad and lodged a complaint to him saying that Narayan Joshi Belsara wanted to take his virtti forcibly from him. So he requested the officer to decide the case in his favour. He further made a demand to Khan that the case of disputed watan should be referred to the Pandhari. On his request Walikhan, the hawaldar of Saswad gave his consent to send the case to the Pandhari which was a community court. Then the hawaldar also asked Narayan Joshi, the father of defendant, whether he would be satisfied if the case would be decided by the Pandhari. Upon this, Narayan Joshi replied that he had no objection if the case was referred to the Pandhari for the judgement. Then Khan Azam summoned a meeting of the Pandhari in the temple of Siddheshwar at Belsara which was attended by the Deshmukh, Deshpande, Mahajan, some mirasdars and the balutedars in the village. The members of the majlis (Pandhari) were assembled in the temple to choose as to who was the true mirasdar among those two claimants namely Narayan Joshi and Yem Joshi who sat in the temple before the deity. Then on one day, twelve balutas who assembled in the temple worshipped the deity by placing the leaves before it. The garlands were placed around the necks of the balutas. Then they placed leaves upon the foreheads of the claimants. Thereafter, Khan asked the balutas to tell him the name of the real claimant whom they know as the true mirasdar. Then the twelve balutas who entered the temple of Moteshwar, brought Yem Joshi Khadiya as true mirasdar from the temple and presented him before Khan.[11] The final judgement on this dispute of watan seems to have given by the Hazir Majlis of Jejuri after forty-five years i.e. in the year of 1677 A.D., of King Shivaji's rule. The dispute was begun during the year of 1631. The Hazir Majlis[12] convened at Jejuri was attended by the government officers such as hawaldar, the Majumdar, Shete and Mahajan etc. The dispute on Joshi and Kulkarni watan and Jejuri Dhalewadi and other villages began by the forefathers of Babaji Parashram, Naro–Somnath Vitthal Ganesh Khade and Baje Gau and it continued among their sons and grandsons too. The dispute was finally settled in February, 1677 A.D., with the consultation of Sabha Naik, Rajmudra and Gota of Mauje Jejuri as described below. It was decided that some of the rights of the watan were to be equally divided among three men and they were to be equally enjoyed by them. The members in whose presence the above decision was announced by the majlis were :

Rajmudra

Vishwanath hawaldar — Trimbak Bapuji Majumdar

Janoji, Krishnaji, Deokoji — Mokadams

Girjoji Desh Setiya,
Rama Setiya
Somaji Mahajan

The subhedar was the highest authority in the subha. When the subhedar desired to settle a dispute, the court which he convened for giving the judgement was also known as Huzur Hazir Majlis. The meeting of the majlis was presided over by the subhedar. A meeting of Huzur Hazir Majlis held at the fort Kondana Mahal was presided over by Dadaji Kondadev, the Subhedar of said Mahal in January 1641 A.D. The Subhedar who convened the Hazir Majlis was attended by Government officers, the watandars such as hawaldar, Deshmukh, Deshkulkarni, Majumdar and Mokadams, Shete and Mahajan etc., of the pargana. The Huzur Hazir Majlis prepared the mahzar on 14th January Thursday, 1641 A.D. It decided the dispute of Sarmakadami between Bhikaji Naikji Dimale of mauje Siware, pargana Khedebare and Naikji Tanaji Dimala of Mauje Kalyan. Bhikaji Dimale and Naikji Dimala, both the persons appeared to the Subhedar and told him that they would be satisfied with the decision given by the Hazir Majlis. The Hazir Majlis summoned to administer justice consulted the Deshmukh of the pargana. Bapuji Tulaji and

Kanaji Jakhoji Kode, the Deshmukhs of Khedebare reported that the father of Bhikaji was enjoying the right over Sarmokadami of Kalyan Taluka. Naikji Dimala had no claim over the Mokadami of said mauje. Other Deshmukhs also supported the cause of Bhikaji Dimala by remaining present as the witnesses to the decision taken by the Deshmukh of pargana. Thus, the Subhedar heard the suit of disputed watan and tried it through the majlis. The majlis gave the verdict that Naikji Dimala had nothing to do with the mokadami because his claim over the watan proved to be false. Therefore, all the rights and perquisites of Sarmokadami of Kalyan Taluka were ordered to be restored to Bhikaji Dimala by the Subhedar of the fort Kondana mahal.[13]

Another dispute[14] regarding the mokadami was also settled by Huzur Hazir majlis, headed by Dadaji Kondadev, the Subhedar of the fort Kondana mahal in February 1643 A.D. There arose a dispute between Zunzarrao Sambhaji Devakate and Bahiraji Mugutrao Sidoji of mauje Mekhali, over the mokadami of the said village. They appeared before the Subhedar and made a complaint regarding their claim over the mokadami. The Subhedar wanted to administer justice to them by summoning a meeting of the Gota. The Gota decided that Bahraji Mugutrao had no concern with the mokadami of Mekhali. Then a dispute on mokadami of mauje Jalochi began between Hatkarrao and Bahiraji Mugutrao. The Subhedar, with the help of Deshmukh and the Gota tried the case. In the light of the justice, administered by the members of the majlis, Mugutrao was granted to enjoy half of the watan of mokadam of Jalochi and remaining half of the watan was distributed between Khandoji Devaji Malgaud and Ramaji Devakate. Bahiraji Mugutrao's claim over the mokadami of Mekhali was denied. The Hazir Majlis of Supe pargana, summoned on 13 Suddha Falgun, Shake 1564 (i.e. on 21st February 1643 A.D.) prepared the mahzar declaring its above stated verdict. The majlis presided over by Dadaji

Kondadev, was also attended by the following prominent persons whose names are listed below :

Bahilimkhan Hawaldar, Baramati Pargana Supe	Krishnaji Kanho Majamdar, Kasba Baramati
Deshmukh Deshkulkarni	Pargana Supe
Baramati Pargana Supe	Vitthal Mahadev
Mokadams	Deshkulkarni
Bakoji and Hiroji Deshmukh	*Mokadams of Supe Pargana*
Ratnoji Mokadam mauje Malgaon	Hiroji Gaud, Malharaji
Bapuji, Nagoji, Sambhaji Baledar	Mahakoji, Tukoji Gaud
Sabaji Hasaji Satwaji,	Malseth Setiya,
Baramati Pargana Supe	Dad Chaugula

Sometimes the Huzur Hazir Majlis was convened by the Subhedar at Kasba place to solve the dispute over the seniority rights of mehatarki. Dadaji Kondadev, presiding over the meeting of the majlis, convened it at Kasba Khed on 14 Shuddha, Jeshta, Shaka 1564. The dispute over the seniority rights of Mehatarki was begun between Yeka Kumbhar and Kau Sau Kumbhau of Poona Pargana. The dispute was centred round the mehatarki of the claimants of Poona. Both the persons took their dispute to the Subhedar of fort Kondana mahal. They appeared before the officer by making the statements that the balutas of the Kasba were knowing about the seniority rights of mehatarki and they would be satisfied if the balutas were consulted for deciding the case. On their request, the Subhedar invited the following persons the balutas to attend the Huzur majlis of Kasba Khed.[15]

Kazi Abdulla Kazi Mahmud pargana Poona Bapuji Mudgal hawaldar pargana Poona (seal)	Rajshri Dadaji Kondadevand the subhedar, fort Kondana (seal)
Maloji Narsingrau and	Sundar Hari Majumdar
Vithoji Sitole Deshmukh	Bapuji and Kanoji Deshmukh, Khedebare
Haibatrao and Balaji	
Deshmukh, Gunjanmawal	Mokadam of mauje Lonikalabhor
Mhakoji Tuka, Mokadam	Mankoji Setiya Poona
Ganseth Setiya, Mahajan	Babaji Seth Mahajan
Peth Shehapura	
Jotisi Kak Patala Joshi	Mahadseti Setiya Peth Murtajabad
Wal Dharna Gurav,	Som Sutar Dorala
Dhaka Mahala Nhavi	Changoji Sutar (Carpenter)
Jamana Mahar Mokadam, mauje Didhi	Vail Varata Parit (Washerman)
	Mauje Yerdwane

On examining the documents, it was found that Yeka was the son of Walhe who was the original person of the family. Yeka had his elder son who was called as Walhe.

His younger son was Kau whose son was Sau. Sau's son was also called as Kau. Thus, the elderness went to Walhe and youngerness seemed to have belonged to Kau. The successor from the house of Yeka would claim above, the right of Mehatarki. The Hazir Majlis called Kau to remain present before the meeting. The majlis asked Kau to give his evidence on the issue. Kau replied that Walhe was the descendant of elder Walhe and hence he might enjoy the seniority right over mehatarki. The majlis with the consultation of the balutas, gave its verdict that the right of mehatarki would be equally divided and would be equally enjoyed by Walhe and Kau Sau. But the seniority right over the Mehatarki would be enjoyed by the house of Walhe who was the descendant of the elder person. The Hazir Majlis which declared the judgement on the dispute of mokadam of mauje Kodit of Poona pargana, between Babaji Nelekar and Janaji Khaira, was summoned and headed by Dadaji Kondadev, the Subhedar of the Fort Kondana on 12 Vadya Shake 1560 and was attended by the following prominent persons.[16]

Deshmukh and Deshak	*Deshmukh and Mokadam*
Bapuji Haibatrao	Babaji Haibatrao and Baji Naik
Babaji Zunjarrao Deshmukh	Babaji Adalrao Deshmukh
Malharaji Deshmukh	Moroji Mokadam
Mokadams	Mauje Pariche
Daspatil mauje Hiware	Baji Mokadam
Mauji Mokadam Mauje Nigade	Mauje Diwadi
Rakuji Mokadam	Sonaji Mokadam
Mauje Ketkawale	Mauje Kambare

Babaji Nelekar of mauje Kodit of Poona pargana was enjoying the right of mokadami. He sold half of the

mokadami to Janajikhaira. But very soon, the dispute regarding the right over the village began between Babaji and Janaji. Babaji wanted to take back the half of mokadami from Janoji Khaira and desired to hand over it to Radraji Jadhav. But Janaji refused to give his right over half of the mokadami. Therefore, Balaji and Rudraji Jadhav both began to fight unitedly with Janoji Khaira and they brought upon him the pressure to give up right over half of the mokadami, sold to him by Babaji. Then the dispute was taken to the Gota. The Gota of the village could not be satisfied with the evidence brought by Khaira and it thought it necessary to try this case by asking him to perform an ordeal. The request of the Gota was respected by Khaira who had performed an ordeal successfully before the members of the majlis in the temple of Shrideva, mahasthal at mauje Mohori Narsapur of Gunjanmawal taluka. Thereafter, as per the decision of the Gota, half of the Mokadami of Babaji was restored to Janaji Khaira. But very soon the dispute on the Mokadami began between Babaji and Rudraji. Then, the dispute was settled by the majlis by declaring that other half share of Babaji's Mokadami should be divided between Krishnaji, the nephew of Babaji and Rudraji. Accordingly, Babaji who possessed nine chavar of land, granted four and half chavar to Khaira and remaining four and half chavar of land was divided equally between his nephew and Rudraji.

In 1650 A.D., we get the next decision on the dispute of mokadamship of mauje Supe between Nilkanthrao, Badal Lakade and Katkar, accorded by the Hazir majlis. The Mahzar was prepared by the majlis, wherein Shamaraji and Sambhajirai Kot Deshmukh, Sakho Gomdeu, Deshkulkarni Mudhaji Baji hawaldar, Yadavaji Majumdar, Gomaji and Vithoji Seti Settya, Shankarrao Gaudi mokadam of Majgaon, Sakhoji Govada, mokadam of mauje Vagaj, Gangaji Khalate, the mokadam of mauje Rataran, Malharaji, Mhaskaji, Ratanaji Baboji Chaugule of Loni, Ramaji Atole Gaudi mokadam of Sirasfal, Sauji and Maluji Khomane Gaudi, mokadam of Malbalbujumkh,

Atale mokadam of mauje Gonabavi, Kankaji Tavira mokadam mauje Abi, Fauji Khomana, mokadam of mauje Kolambave, Kanhoji and Malaji Bhadkar, mokadam of mauje Tardoli, Nakeli Nagoji Nawadikar, Deshmukh, taluka Khedebare etc., were present. The case was about the job of mokadamship of mauje Supe. The dispute began between Badal Lakade and Katkar regarding the mokadamship of said village. It was stated that Lakade had left the village and in his absence, the mokadamship of mauje Supe was enjoyed by Katkar. But due to devastating condition of the village, he could not collect the amount due from peasants. He could earn ten to twenty hons as income from the village previously. But later on, it became impossible for him to send the stipulated amount to Government treasury. The circumstances compelled him to sell his half of the perquisites of the mokadamship to God Gawada Rod. The remaining half share of his mokadamship, was enjoyed by Katkar. After some years, Katkar could not manage to pay the government dues. Therefore, he sold out half of his share of the mokadamship to Nilkanthrao Gosawi. Thus, the mokadamship of mauje Supe was distributed among three men. The half of the mokadamship belonged to Nilkanthrao and Katkar, and other half was enjoyed by God Gawada. But later on God Gawada ran away on account of non-payment of government dues. But the same sum was paid by Kate Deshmukh who in return got half of the mokadamship belonging to God Gawada. Then God Gawada collected one hundred and fifty hons from the peasants in tarf under his jurisdiction. He again enjoyed half share of the mokadamship by receiving it from Kate Deshmukh. The plaintiff (Nilkanthrao) petitioned to the officer of Supe pargana for proper justice. Because Katkar had attacked God Gawada's claim over the mokadamship. The officer wanted to decide the case by transferring it to the Gota of the village. The members of the Gotasabha assembled there gave the decision that the mokadamship of the said village was to be divided among Nilkanthrao, Katkar and God Gawada. Moreover, the income earned from the mokadamship was equally borne by three persons. The decision given by the local body satisfied all of them and they accepted it happily. Every one of them gave in writing to each other that every person was to live the life peacefully by enjoying only his own share of the mokadamship.[17] The Hazar Majalas met at Bamnoli to decide the dispute over the mokadami watan of mauje Salasi among Aloji Jasojirao Muslim Kandatkar, Tanaji Chandroji Kandatkar and Dharoji Kandatkar. The quarrel between their families for the mokadami rights was continued since three generations. When King Shivaji conquered Jawali, it was he who gave an order to the Subhedar to settle the dispute. The plaintiffs appeared before the Subhedar and made a complaint against Alojirao Muslim Kandatkar regarding the rights of Mokadami watan. Alojirao Jasojirao wrote the plaint to the Subhedar his forefathers were enjoying the rights over the mokadami watan of mauje Salasi. He told the chief officer of the Subha Jawali, that the dispute be decided by resorting to the Rava ordeal. He gave his consent to the Subhedar to pass through this ordeal for settling of the case. Chandraji Khandatkar and Dharojirao Khandatkar were sent to that for an ordeal. The plaintiff had to perform an ordeal before the Hazar Majalas and the hawaldar of Bamnoli. He passed through the Rava ordeal before the goddess Hanmant. Having taken an oath before the goddess of Hanmant, Alojirao Jasojirao passed through the ordeal, but he could not escape without injury and failed in performing an ordeal successfully, Therefore, the claims of Alojirao over the said Mokadaji watan declared to be false. The rights over the watan were granted to Tanajirao Chandrajirao Khandatkar and Dharojirao Khandatkar. The mahzar was declared and prepared by the Hazar Majalas on 3rd day of Vadya Margasis, Shaka 1579. The members who attended the Hazar Majalas were as follows :

The subhedars such as Gorkhoji Dinkarrao Kakade, Visaji Naganath, and the Mahajan of Kasba Jawali,

Ganashet Shete, Silversmith of Jawali etc. Other persons who attended the meeting of the Majalas were such as Antaji Sindhanath, hawaldar, Shankaraji Naganath Majumdar, Maloji Godawe Desai. The Gardeshaks of Bamnoli such as Anaji Ranganath hawaldar Sar Deshmukh, Visodev Kulkarni, Changoji Bamane mokadam, Valaji Ambaji Angode Desai, Dadaji Kondaba Kulkarni, Babaji Rikama mokadam, Kondaji Pakoji Kadam, Sonaji Jambala, Malaji Honaji Kadam etc. The Deshaks of tarf Tambi who remained present there, were Krishnaji, Ratnaji Balaji, Hiroji Yesaji, the mokadams of village Akalape, the mokadams of mauje Ahrr. The metakars of the villages of Falani mauje Kas, Matha Valawan, Kolghar, the mokadams of Kandatkhore, Athegaon, the Shepherds and the village mahars of villages like Bamnoli, Akalape, Arav, Niwali, Lamaj, Pimpari, Sindhi, Tambi etc., also attended the meeting of the majlis.[18]

In 1661 A.D., there arose a dispute between Mahadaji Vadjoji Randiwe and Godaji Jauji Pachputa of mauje Bhawali over the mokadamship of said village. Mahadaji Ranadiwe appeared before Raje Palkar, the Sarnobat, the Subhedar of Poona Pargana, and lodged a complaint against Godaji Jauji Pachputa. The Mahzar prepared the majlis attended by the Mokadams, Mahajans and artisans of the villages of Khadale, Navegau, Vadgau, Kesurdi, Belake, Bhawali, Loni Palsi, Sangawi etc., of Poona Pargana gives an account of the nature of the dispute tried by the Huzur Majlis, with the help of the Gota as given below. The mokadamship and the right of mirasi of mauje Bhawali were enjoyed by Godaji Pachputa. But those rights were challenged by Mahadaji Randiwe. The plaintiff made a request to the Subhedar to issue him an order to restore the mirasi watan of the village Bhawali to him. He stated to the officer that during the days of famine, Godaji Jauje, the mokadam of mauje Bhawali, sold his mokadamship to Somaji Pachputa. The Gota of Bhawali in Shirwal pargana prepared the document, showing Somaji's claim of Mokadamship on 6th day of Krishna Paksha, in month of Chaitra, Shaka 1557. Then the mokadams of villages such as Godaji Patil, Gomaji Patil, Esoji Patil, Pilajee Patil, Emaji Patil etc., who went to Ozarade village told that Abaji Pachputa the father of Somaji was enjoying the mirasi right over mauje Anewadi and they offered him the mirasi right of mauje Bhawali. The members of the Gota who were present at Kulwadi and attended the meeting were Naikaji Naik, Maloji Raje and Sambhaji Desai etc. Other men such as Kashi Vishwanath Yaranda, Godava Digha and the Kulkarni Mulhai of Songirwadi etc. were present as the gohidars. The document prepared by the Gota revealed that the mokadamship and the mirasi of the said village was the privilege of the father of Somaji and he enjoyed it for more than sixteen or seventeen years. Later on he left the village, went to the place where Abaji was residing. He got the document prepared by the Gota of that place. The same document was kept in the house of Somaji Pachputa and was presented it before the Hazir majlis. The Hazir majlis referred to the case to the Gota of mauje Pimpale, near Saswad of Poona pargana and administered the justice that the right of mokadamship of mauje Bhawadi should be restored to Somaji Abaji Pachputa. His rights over cultivable land and also over the populated part of village called pandhari land were to be enjoyed by him. This decision was given in presence of goddess Bahirav Shripipaleshwar, who was regarded as the witness to it. Other persons who gave their witnesses to the decision were the following members of the Gota of mauje Pimpale[19] (near Saswad) :

Malnath Mahar, Mauje Pimpale	Godaji Patil, Dhangare
Malaji Nalwada	mokadam mauje Khurd
Bhanaji Jauji Hatir (painter of Saswad)	Baloji Chaugula Bhika (Saswad)

Sabaji Waikar, Mauje Bopegaon of Poona pargana	Kanhoram Dani Saswad

The Hazir Majlis which decided the case of the patilkiwatan on 10th October, 1675 was presided over by Mahadaji Samraj, the Subhedar and Mawal pargana and was attended by following prominent officers and watandars such as Mahadaji Narsinh Prabhu, the hawaldar of Mawal pargana, Jaitaji Naik Malharji Naik Karajawane Deshmukh of pargana Rajshri, Udhoram Sarmajumdar, Sonaji Tamaji Prabhu Majumdar, Jauji Arojoji Surawa, mauje, the mokadam of mauje Vadadare. Other mokadams who were present in the majlis were Lonkar of mauje Kopare, Tanaji Pokala of mauje Dhairi, Bhikaji Bhagat of Khurd Sawane, Tukoji Nalaga of Vadgaon, Miraji Musalman of mauje Katraj, Malaji of Madhave, Babaji Kanada Bapaji Narsingrao of Lawale, Vithoji Jori Payeghude, Malharaji Khradi of mauje Gorhe Budruk, Chimanaji Bapuji of Nadosi, Rekhoji Chindha of Ambegaon, Siuji mokadam of Vadgaon, Honaji Veda of Bawadhan Sauji Patil of Barhata, Hiraji Tammura of mauje Kotharud, Babaji Patil, Jauji Patil, Bhika Patil of mauje Yere, Bapuji Sawar, Rayaji Ranwada of the villages Chande and Nande respectively. The mahzar declared that mokadamship of mauje Khambagaon in Mawal pargana belonged to Lohkar. But he sold it to Payegude Deshmukh who gave it to the King. But King Shivaji granted it as award to Bakaji Farjand. In its return, the king asked Bakaji to perform the job of Patilki of the said village. King Shivaji also issued an order to the Gotasabha attending it by prominent persons and balutas of the villages to prepare the mahzar. On receiving the order from Shivaji, the Gota prepared the mahzar authorising Bakaji Farjand's claim over the mokadami watan of the said village. The Gota also mentioned in the mahzar that after the death of Bakaji, his sons or daughters would be the claimants of the watan. Even if Bakaji would have no male issue, his daughter's husband would enjoy the Patil watan. The Khurdkhat as was suggested by King Shivaji, was prepared by the Gota. Thus, after preparing of the Mahzar, following persons were the witnesses to it and also affixed their designations on it.[20]

Witnesses

Abade Bhat Thakar Joshi	Rayaji Vitthal, Malhar Dado, Satputa, Kulkarni
Umaji Ganoji Walguda, Chaugula	Hiroji Bhadiraga
Jauji Baji Ram Sutar	Bop Varata, Dhar Varata, Washerman Babaji Kaloji, Oilman Gota Mahar Virtikar Mahar

The King also informed the Subhedar, Deshmukh, and the mokadams of the pargana Mawal that the Patilki watan of the said village has been granted to Bakaji Farjand by himself. The cases of religious dispute were also brought before the Hazir Majlis which administered the justice to the persons appearing before it. The religious dispute regarding the purification of the person was settled by the Hazir Majlis of Nasik, which met on 8th October, 1641. Sona Prabhu, the Dharmadhikari appeared in the court of the King and made a complaint against Gana Shukla that the latter prohibited him from taking meals along with him and other Brahmin persons. He, therefore, petitioned to the King to remove the unjustice done on him and decide as to whether allegations levelled against him were true or false by summoning the meeting of the Hazir Majlis. He also appealed to the King to summon Gana Shukla for appearance in the court of justice. The King gave an order to the pargana officer to decide the case. Then the officer summoned the meeting of the Hazir Majlis attended by the prominent Brahmin persons to give the decision on this case. The plaintiff who was present before the majlis narrated the detailed account of his case as mentioned below.

The plaintiff was staying in Jawar tarf of Konkan region for some days. During the period of his stay, he ate rice washed and cleaned by the Shudra person. Thus, Sona Prabhu became impure by eating rice cooked by the Sudraman. With an aim of purifying himself, he approached to Dinkarbhat and other Brahmins. Dinkarbhat who was resident of Kashi, had come at Nasik and gave advice to Sonaprabhu to undergo the penance at Jawar. On the advice of Dinkarbhat, Sonaprabhu performed the penance and became purified. On hearing of the statements of the plaintiff, the Hazir Majlis attended by the Brahmins of Nasik, gave the verdict that Sonaprabhu had undergone the penance and declared him as purified.[21]

A remarkable case and the judicial decision declared by Huzur Hazir Majlis met at Gulshanabad is found in our records and its brief account has been given below. The dispute arose in 1646 A.D. between Sona Prabhu and Mahadu Prabhu, Dharmadhikarni of the mamla Gulshanabad and Siubhat, was over the right of the Dharmadhikarni. The Huzur Hazir Majlis[22] convened at Nasik prepared the Mahzar which gave decision on the issue. The majlis was headed by the Deshmukh and was attended by the Kazi Syed, Asharaf, Amin Visaji Ram, Kukundaji Vishnu, Deshmukh of tarf Monadi, Trimbak Gopinath, the Deshpande of pargana, Siwaji Anant Kulkarni, and Krishnaji Bokoji Patil Krishnaji Patil, the mokadam of Nasik, the Hejib like Krishnaji Bokoji Patil, Namaji Balal, Sabaji Sido Balal, Shete Mahajan, Basavseti, Nauseti etc. The Dharmadhikarni such as Sonaprabhu, Mahadu Prabu etc., approached the Hazir Majlis and made a complaint with it, that Siubhat was prohibiting them from enjoying the right of Dharmadhikarni. He did not allow Jakhoji Chiloji Sonar of mauje Chandwad to perform the Sanskaras like Panigrahana with the help of

Dharmadhikarni on the occasion of marriage ceremony celebrated at his house. Siubhat also enjoyed the right over jotisi vritti of Kasba Chandwad. When son Prabhu was prohibited by Siubhat from performing the Sanskaras of Panigrahana and Sewantipuja at the marriage ceremony of a daughter of Jakhoji Chiloji Sonar, the former lodged a complaint against the latter to the Diwan's office. He also reported the matter to the Government officers like Amin and Sekadar of the pargana. Then the officer gave an order to Sona Prabhu to perform the Panigrahana Sanskara on the marriage occasion. Sona Prabhu, on receiving the order, performed the Panigrahana in the marriage ceremony. But Siubhat got annoyed and he fought with Sona Prabhu. Therefore, Sona Prabhu lodged a complaint against him to the Deshmukh and Deshpande of the pargana and convened a meeting of the majlis for giving the verdict on the said issue. The majlis which prepared the mahzar declared that the right of Dharmadhikarni was to be enjoyed by Sona Prabhu Mahadu Prabhu etc. The rights of performing the Ganesh worship, Kalash worship and Panigrahana etc., were restored to them as their hereditary claims over that watan also.[23]

BRAHMASABHA

The body of learned Brahmins met at holy places of the Hindus was called as Brahmasabha. This assembly used to interpret controversial matters socio-religious in nature. For understanding the composition, powers and functioning of the Brahmasabha some notable disputes decided by this assembly and described below, are found in our documents. The Brahmasabha that met on Shuddha Pratipada Shaka 1492 of the month of Jeshta, at Kolhapur to decide the dispute between Posibhat Latikar and Virpakshabhat Vedanti regarding the rights of village Upadhya, consisted of the members such as Timanbhat Gotkhindkar, Narsinh Pathak, Upadhya Aste, Godaba Bhaluvi, Chandoba Kulkarni, Naron Pandit Devana Pandit, Mudgalbhat, Malibhat Vishwanathbhat,

Damavanbhat, Govind Pathak Pandharpurkar etc., who were present there. Pasibhat Latikar and Virpakshabhat appeared before the government officer and lodged the complaint with him. The officer called the meeting of Brahmasabha which decided the dispute by preparing the mahzar attested by a large number of its members. The Brahmasabha declared that the right of Upadhya over the village did not belong to Rudra Pathak and Pasibhat. Their rights of Upadhya over the village were thus set aside by the assembly. The decision given by Brahmasabha was respected by the Rajmudra.[24] It was presided over by Mahado Ram Peshwa, Rajshri Nisakrau and was attended by Balwantrau Bhaskar, the Majumdar, Ramaji, Thanadar, Sonaji Patel of Patole Shete, Mahajan, Kulkarni, Chaugula, Dhamavanbhat Jotisi, Valvekar Jotisi, Vishwanathbhat, Narasibhat Dharmadhikari of Sirale etc.

Another dispute regarding the watan of Dharmadhikara was also settled by the Brahmasabha. For instance, the Brahmasabha convened at Kolhapur in the temple of Kapaleshwar on 13th Shuddha of Ashadh month, Shaka 1555, to decide the dispute between Joshi and Padam Nabhibhat regarding the watan of Dharmadhikara of mahal Kolhapur.[25] The Kulkarni of mauje Paluskar approached the Dharmadhikari and showed him the document claiming his right over the said watan. Then the case was brought before the government officer. The officer called Joshi and Dharmadhikari before him to give their statements regarding the claim over the watan. Then those documents were given to the Patil of the village who convened the meeting of Brahmasabha in the temple of Shri Maha Laxmi. The members of the assembly asked Madhav Pathak, Linganbhat Ekodikar to prove how the watan belonged to him and how Joshi's claim over the watan was wrong? To this, he answered that the original man of his family was Vishnu Pathak who was granted the watan of five places on the occasion of his marriage ceremony. The members again asked him to show the documents of permission to them.

Then, after two days, the claimant showed his documents to the members. They revealed that since long time, he was enjoying the watan of Dharmadhikara which he got it from his ancestor Achyutbhat and since then, his family was enjoying the same watan. The Brahmasabha declared that the watan of Dharmadhikaran belonged to Padamanabhibhat. The Brahmins present at the time of the decision given by Brahmasabha and who rendered their witnesses were Bapubhat Krishnabhat Bharane, Ram Padhya, Gangadharbhat, Puranik Bandbhat, Godbole, Janibhat Dhawalikar, Madevbhat Urankar, Narsinhbhat Puranik Lakshubhat, Vekadbhat Bapubhat, Valvadekar, Narsibhat, Mudgalbhat etc.[26] The Brahmasabha presided over by Mahado Pandit Deshkulkarni of Kasba Sorati, attended by the learned Brahmins such as Janardhan Bhat Talalbhat, Vishwanathbhat, Shankaraji Pant, Majumdar, Kapilaji Mutalik Kulkarni etc., decided the dispute arose regarding the jotisi Watan and its rights between Narsinh Bhat and Vishwanathbhat. Vishwanathbhat told the members of the assembly that the Brahmasabha met at the holy place of Kurdawadi gave the decision in his favour. He also showed them the letter of decision declared by the Brahmasabha of that place. The Niwadpatra of the Sabha revealed that the watan of Jotisi and Upadhik of the villages Sirati and Hasur were to be enjoyed by Vishwanathbhat. Narsinhbhat was sure that Rameshwaribhat etc., gave in writing to Vishwanathbhat that the said watan was to be equally divided and half share of the watan was granted by them to the latter. The Brahmasabha of Mangalvedhe gave its verdict by allowing Vishwanathbhat to enjoy half of the Jotisi watan of those villages.[27] The Brahamsabha presided over by Rajshri Keshavaji Naik Deshmukh met at Wai decided the dispute between vedic scholar Narsinhbhat and other vedic scholars Narayanbhat and Shankarbhat regarding vritti and Inam land of one and half chavar. Narsinhbhat approached the Brahmasabha of Wai, and made a complaint that his brothers also claimed over the Inamland granted to him. On hearing the complaint, the Deshmukh called upon the learned Brahmins of Wai to give their verdict on this issue. The Brahmasabha decided the case on the basis of the rules or the principles embodied in Dharmashastras and in the law book of Vidnyaneshwar. The assembly declared that the relatives of Narsinhbhat had no right over the vritti and the Inamland to be enjoyed by him. Narsinhbhat on the basis of his scholarship was granted the Inamland by the government. His brothers were separated from each other when he got the Inamland. Therefore, they had no right to claim over the Inamland of one and half chavar, of Narsinhbhat who earned it with the help of merit and hard work. The Gotasabha of the place was also consulted for this issue. The Gotasabha also respected the decision given by the Brahmasabha and gave its consent that the vritti and the Inamland should be enjoyed only by Narsinhbhat[28] and other persons wrongly claimed over it. The Brahmasabha also examined the dispute arose between Hindu and Muslim litigants. In January 1611 A.D., there arose a dispute between Narsoji Jagdale Deshmukh and Bapaji Yakubaji Musalman of Kasba Masur over the Patilwatan of the said Kasba. The case was tried and decided for twice before it was brought to the Brahmasabha of Kasba Pratishthan. But those decisions satisfied neither of the litigants, hence the case was taken to the Brahmasabha convened at Kasba Pratishthan. The Hindu and Muslim litigants had brought the letters from the native hawaldar with whom they had lodged the complaint and produced them before the hawaldar at another place. The thalkari hawaldar examined those documents and called a meeting of Brahmasabha to administer the justice to the litigants. The Brahmasabha met at Kasba Pratishthan was presided over by the Dharmadhikari who examined those letters and administered the justice on the basis of the principles embodied in the law book of Vidnyaneshwar. It declared that the Muslim person's claim over the Patil watan as false and illegal.[29] Thus, the dispute regarding the Patil watan between the Hindu and Muslim litigants was decided by the Brahmasabha. In October 1656 A.D., we find that a meeting of the Brahmasabha was called to give the decision on the dispute arose between two communities of Lingayat and Jain of the Peth Athani.[30] The men belonging to the Lingayat community lodged a complaint against the Jain men that the latter criticised Jangam Dev, the guru of the Lingayat people. The Jain people gave an answer to this, that Jangam Khelata blamed their Jain Guru and his followers. But the Lingayat men replied to them by saying that Jangam was speaking according to Vedashastra and therefore, he could not be held responsible for the allegation levelled against him by the Jain followers. Thus, a dispute arose between both the communities who approached Abdul Ali, the hawaldar of Athani for summoning of a meeting of the learned vedic scholars of the Brahmasabha for giving the opinion on the said dispute. The Jain persons such as Jain Khumache Silas Upadhya Seti Sagal, Cheni Setikar of Shahapur etc., were sent to Kashi to invite the learned scholars expert in Shaddarshana. The Brahmasabha was to consult those experts and take advice from them for administering the justice. Mahaldar, Lingoji Jito, mauje Soli Gangisethi Peth Joharapur, Lingappa Aaki, Yalappa Aadiki, Jobi Seti Setikar Peth Joharapur, Sidwir Seti Bonu Sindana Ravirau Desai of pargana Jambkhandi, Ramaji Apaji Deshmukh, Vekatardi Trimal Pandit, Sindana Bhupati Desai, Sidgunda Liganda Desai, Patel of Athani, Sidganda Chaudhari, etc. The majlis prepared the mahzar which reveals that some men of Lingayat Mahanad of Peth Athani had arrived at Jambkhandi and they summoned all the members of Government clerks, Desai, Deshkulkarni, Patel, Chaudhari, Patanseti and Mahajan Seti, alongwith all other Kunbis and balutas of the pargana to give justice on the dispute between the Jain community and Lingayat men. The members were asked to give their opinion on the procession by which the Jain teacher and the teacher of

Lingayat Mahanad were brought to the peth. The members such as Sindana Bhupati Desai, Sidgauda Desai, Ramaji Apaji Deshkulkarni, Nagoda Patel, Sidgauda Chaudhari, Lingiseti, Palaneti, Nagappa Jain Mahajan and other twelve balutas assembled there replied that the practice of carrying the teacher of Lingayat Mahanad in procession through the streets was observed by the Lingayat community. They also told that the Jain people did not observe the practice of bringing their teacher to the town by way of taking him in procession through the streets accompanied by the Jain followers.[31] Huzur Hazir Majlis met in the temple of goddess Hanumant, of pargana Jambkhandi was headed by Hawaldar and was attended by Apaji Mahadev, Ramaji Bhimaji, the majumdar, Shankaraji Mahaldar, Karappa Nandirau Desai, Chengaud Patel mauje Kotalagi, Longoji Jito Kulkarni of mauje Kotalagi etc., Sindana Desai, Sidgauda Desai, Ramaji Apaji Deshkulkarni, Nadgaud Patel, Sidgauda Chaudhari Shete, Mahajan and twelve balutas of the kasba Athani gave a complaint that the men belonging to Lingayat Mahanad of pargana Jambkhandi reported to them that the persons belonging to Jain Khuma had gone to Kashi.

The Lingayat men had brought with them a letter of decision from Kashi. They had made a request to call the Deshak and the Diwan for deciding the case. Hence, the government officers, and the members of the Gotasabha were also assembled. At that time the Jain men did not speak about the Jayapatra. But after five months, the Jain teacher and some of his followers had brought it with them. They were asked to remain present before the government officer and all other members of the body. The men belonging to Lingayat were also called upon to be present there. But the latter refused to remain present before the Patel of Yenapur.[32] Then on 30th December, 1658, the Huzur Hazir Majlis was summoned. The prominent members who attended it were, Shankarji. The majlis declared its vertict that the Lingayat of Mahanad should only bring their guru to the peth by way of taking him in procession. But the majlis did not grant the permission to the Jain people to observe the above mentioned practice.[33] The majlis which administered the justice to the Lingayat people was attended by Dadaji Vekatardi Pandit hawaldar, majumdar, Desai, Ramaji Apaji Deshkulkarni, Sidgauda Ligauda Patel, Sidgauda Chaudhari of peth Athani of mamale Mahamadapur convened on 14th December, 1670 A.D., decided that the Jain community was not entitled to enjoy the right to take the procession by carrying a pot with a lotus flower. The same right of taking procession was granted to the Lingayat men of Mahanad only.[34] To decide the dispute regarding the Upadhya vritti between Golawalikar Padhyes and Devarukhe Brahmin, a great assembly[35] consisting of learned Pandits such as Kavindra Paramananda, Ananta, Mahadeva Sesa etc., was held by King Shivaji at Rajapur in 1664 A.D. Thus, the assembly of learned Pandits used to decide the religious suits.

REFERENCES AND FOOTNOTES

1. SPSS, II, Letter No 1907
2. SCS, III, Letter No. 439
3. Ibid, III, PP. 53-54
4. Sanada Patre, Prakaran No. 4, Lekha No. 9, quoted in Gune V. T., JSM, PP. 188-189
5. MIS, XVII, Lekh No. 10
6. Dev S. S. Shri Ramdasi Sanshodhan, Part II, P. 11, also see Gune V. T., Op cit, PP. 197-198
7. SCS, IX, Lekh No. 66. This Mahazarnama though belongs to the year 1685-86 of King Sambhaji's regime, it helps us to understand the nature of King's Rajmandal.
8. SPSS. II, Letter No. 1984
9. Gune V. T., Op cit, P. 35
10. SCS. 7, Letter No. 21
11. Ibid 7, PP. 33-34
12. Ibid 7, Letter No. 58
13. Ibid 7, Letter No. 31
14. Ibid 7, Letter No. 32
15. Ibid III, Letter No. 27
16. Ibid I, Letter No. 26

17. SCS, I, Letter No. 41
18. SCS, III, Letter No. 639
19. SCS, I, Letter No. 49
20. Ibid II, Letter Nos. 281 and 282
21. Ibid II, Letter Nos. 294 and 295
22. Ibid II, Letter No. 297
23. Ibid II, P. 298
24. MIS, XX, Letter No. 185
25. Ibid, XX, Letter No. 186
26. Ibid XX, P. 281
27. SCS, III, Letter No. 631
28. MIS, XX, Letter No. 126
29. Ibid XV, Letter No. 6
30. SCS, II, Letter No. 353
31. Ibid II, Letter Nos. 356 and 357
32. Ibid II, Letter No. 355
33. Ibid II, P. 358
34. Ibid II, Letter No. 359
35. Bendre V. S., Dandaniti, PP. 30-31

4

Gotamajlis

We have a large number of evidences about the exact nature, composition and functioning of the Gotamajlis of Shivaji's period. The Gotamajlis decided the civil disputes brought before it by taking into consideration many important aspects involved in the suit and also by examining all the written documents or oral evidences regarding those cases.

At village level, the Gotamajlis[1] consisted of Deshak like Deshmukh, taksimdar, Sarkhot, Shete Naik and mokadams, oilman, potter, washerman, and mahar etc. The Gotamajlis of Dhanib in taluka Kanadkhore was held on 24th January 1667 A.D. to decide a dispute regarding the distribution of family property between two persons, Babaji Deshmukh and Maloji Patangrao who had blood relations with each other. The Gotamajlis was presided over by King's mother and was attended by vedic scholar of mamle Rair, Dhaniba, Bhagat Koli, Teli Mahatariya Gurav Salvi potter, Mahar and many mokadams of the villages of Kanadkhore taluka. The Gotamajlis tried the watan cases by going through all the written records made available to it by the parties involved in the dispute. For instance, the Gotamajlis which was attended by the Deshkulkarni of Mawal, Jaitaji Naik, Malharaji Naik Deshmukh and the mokadams like Babaji, Jauji Bhika

Bapuji Patil of the villages of Kotharud, Yere, Chande etc., respectively was summoned to prepare the mahzar for declaring that the patil watan of mauje Khamgaon of Mawal taluka was granted as gift by King Shivaji to Bakaji Bhosale for his loyalty to the ruler. The mahzar prepared by the Gotamajlis declared its decision that long back, the patil watan of mauje Khamgaon belonged to Kadim Lohar who sold out it to Payagude Deshmukh. But it was purchased by Shivaji from Payagude. And then, King Shivaji granted it to Bakaji Farjand Bhosale as present.[2] The above record mentions that the Gotamajlis which prepared mahzar, granted the patil watan of village to Bakaji and examined earlier documents gone through those written documents, which were issued to the Gotamajlis by King Shivaji. A quarrel between Lumaji Tejaji Botare and Kondaji Lakhamoji Takawane of mauje Pargaonmala of taluka Patas of Pune prant, came up before King Shivaji. The plaintiff Lumaji Botare made a complaint to the King against Lakhmaji Takawane that the latter killed six persons and was creating obstacle in his right of enjoying of patil watan. After hearing of the complaint, King Shivaji issued an order to the Ramaji Balal, the hawaldar of Karhepathar Saswad, to decide the dispute between two parties. The hawaldar sent an order to Gotamajlis to decide the case. The subhanaiki summoned the meeting of the Gotamajlis and called the brothers of Takawane to remain present before the Gota. Lumaji Botare was also present on that occasion. The Gotamajlis consisting of Zamindars, Deshmukh, Deshkulkarni, Shete, of pargana Saswad, the mokadams such as Konoji Bele of Khanwadi, Yekaji Dirirajar Ganoji of Vanpuri, Trimbakaji Darekar of mauje Ambalnime, Vithoji Taware of mauje Moragaon, Kamaji Nazarekar, Kauji Bankar of Niluj, Lakhamoji Bhagat of mauje Rajori, Nagoji Kamate of Seur, Apaji Dilek Kodaji Akarase of Majwadi, Jawaji Khedekar of Gulbheri, Tukoji Jagtap. Tanaji Chaugula, Ramaji Hade, Ramaji, Baluji Borkar, and many such other mokadams of villages in Pune Prant.[3] When

Takawan was brought before the Gotasabha, the members of the Gota asked him the cause for creating the disturbance to Botare. Then the Gotasabha also took in writing the complaints, rajiname, and Katabe etc., from each party. By going through the evidences the Gota reached the decision that Takawane who was also a Watandar had committed three murders of the balutas of village Bhowar. Therefore, the criminal was punished by the Gota by imposing upon him the penalty of two hundred hons. The Gota also declared that the half of the patil watan of Takawane should be granted to Botare. He also gave the decision that Takawane who was younger to the eldest person, Botare should act accordingly and pay respect to him.[4] In connection with the functioning and power of Gota, the evidence found in the contemporary record is of special interest to our readers. According to the document, the Gota of the village in Wai pargana was presided over by Kanho Pandit, the Hawaldar, and was attended by the members such as Nago Trimal Pant Majumdar, Narokanho, Najarkhan, Vitthal Krishna Chitnis, Keshavji Naik Desai, Sambseti Setiya, Krishnaji Shet, Abaji Chaudhari, Bapuji Setiya and the mokadams of the villages of Wai pargana such as Mohammad Patel, mokadam of Wai, Abaji, Krishnaji of mauje Songirwadi, Tulaji Antaji of mauje Nimb, Naikaji, Kondaji of mauje Arel, Sakhoji, Mangoji, Baji of Koregaon, Ratoji Patel of Tadawale, Suryaji, Yesaji and Bhikaji of mauje Abhepuri, Sidhojipati, Sonaji Patil of Asale, Kaloji, Dadaji of Sindhwadi, Mahimaji Patil of mauje Gove, Kadatoji, Timaji of mauje Dhamnur, Somaji Patil of mauje Pandogadwadi etc., prepared a mahzar at a place as Parsani. The plaintiffs Anaji Lakhmoji and Pilajee, Kanaji Kondaji Mahigude the mokadam of said village made a complaint to the Government officer that the Patil Watan of said village was enjoyed by their forefathers. Kondaji Patel had been enjoying the watan since many years back. During the days of famine, the lands in that village remained uncultivated and Kondaji Patel could not perform the duty of Patel during the famine period as he had left the villages and was migrated to some other place for his livelihood. During the reign of Randullahkhan of Adilshahi rule, Madhavaji Krishna hawaldar of the pargana issued an order to Kondaji that as he failed in performing the duty of the patil, the said watan of mauje Parsani was taken over by the government.[5] Then the sultan granted same watan to Girmaji Trimbak, Suryaji and Sonaji of mauje Mhasave of pargana Kudal and Yewale of mauje Bhogau of pargana Murhe by dividing the right over the patil watan among them. Then, after returning to his native place, Kondaji made a complaint to the Government requesting that the patil watan should be restored to him. But the government officer divided the watan among Kondaji, Girmaji Rikame and Yewale etc. The record speaks of the truth that the Subhedar namely Sarjakhan Muhamad accepted the amount of seven hundred and twenty hons from Rikame and Yewale and in return, he granted each of them, one-third share of the right over patil watan.[6] During the reign of Randullabhkhan, Madhavji Krishana the hawaldar of pargana issued an order to Gangoji Naik Desai to prepare the mahzar. Therefore, the mahzar was prepared. Then a dispute between Kondaji Patil and Rikame and Yewale, arose regarding the right over the patil watan. In the reign of Afzalkhan the hawaldar namely Shamaji Shivdeu reported to the master that Kondaji Patil had left the village. He also applied to Sardesai and Desai to send Kondaji Mr. Rikame and Yewale to Talegaon for deciding the dispute. Accordingly, three persons had gone to Talegaon in kasba Induri where they got the final award (Thalpatra) regarding the patil watan. The Gotamajlis at Talegaon examined the evidences and reached the decision that the right of Mr. Rikame and Yewale over the watan was false. The Gota gave the final award to Kondaji who brought it and showed it to Sardesai and Desai. Then, the mahzar claiming Kondaji's right over the patil watan was prepared. So the defendants made the request to the officer of an appeal to the Gotasabha at Chimangaon. Both were sent to that place whose officer decided the case in favour of Kondaji. But the decision given by the officer at Chimangaon did not satisfy the defendants. Hence they demanded that the decision regarding the patil watan ought to have decided by the Gota. So Baji Ganaji Rikame made a complaint that in the reign of Randullahkhan, the village of Parsani remained barren because Kondaji made no attempt to bring the land under cultivation. During this period, Sonaji Rikame Suryaji and Sonaji Yewale were granted the patil watan of the said village. Sonaji Rikame and Suryaji, Sonaji, Yewale were enjoying one-half share over the watan. But during the reign of Afzalkhan Kondaji made a request that the dispute about the patil watan of village Parsani should be decided by sending him to the Gota at Talegaon in kasba Junnar. Then Kondaji approached the Gota at Talegaon which gave him final award (Thalpatra) about the patil watan and declared that the right of Mr. Rikame and Yewale over that watan was false. The Gota at Talegaon ascertained the truth by examining the evidences and declared that Kondaji's claim over the watan was legal and it decided to restore it to him. The members of Gota at Talegaon who examined the mahzar prepared by the Gota at an earlier place found it as incomplete. The said mahzar did not contain the signatures of the witnesses who were present at the time of dispensing the justice by the Gota. Hence, the Gota at Talegaon declared Kondaji Mahagude as a rightful claimant for the watan of mauje Parsani. The Gota at Talegaon was presided over by Desai mokadam of that village and was attended by Deshkulkarni Shete, Mahajan and other mokadams in kasba Junnar.[7] Similarly when a dispute arose between Pantaji Gopinath Bokil and Vitthal Mahadev and Trimbak Gokhadeu, over the Kulkarni watan of Baramati, the plaintiff made the complaint to the King for deciding the suit. King Shivaji asked his Subhedar, namely Visaji Ballal to hold an enquiry about the matter. King Shivaji also authorised the Subhedar to summon a meeting of Gotasabha to enquire and investigate the case and decide the dispute.[8] The record speaks of the fact that the dispute over the Kulkarni and Deshpande watan between two parties had begun during the reign of Malik Ambar. The same case was also decided during the reign of Randullahkhan. King Shivaji had also dispensed justice in favour of Bokil. The mahzar was also prepared by the authorities. Shahista Khan and Mirza Raja Jaisinh who examined the Sanad bearing the signature of Deshaks and other witnesses decided the case in favour of Bokil and granted him the right over the Deshpande Watan of Baramati pargana. But the opposite party created obstacle to Bokil, in enjoying the rights of said watan. Therefore, the King issued an order to the Subhedar to decide the case with the help of Gota of that place. As the Gota had power of decision, the King asked his officer to refer the case to the Gotamajlis consisting of the Deshaks, mokadams, the balutas and some elder residents of the village. As the record is incomplete, we do not know about the decision given by the Gota over the dispute of above mentioned Deshpande watan.

Even some difficult or most complicated disputes like the distribution of watan among the kinsmen were also settled by the Gotamajlis. Thus, a mahzar[9] of Shaka 1594 on the first day (Padawa) of the month of Shrawan of this year made the distribution of watan among Vithoji Bapuji Barvaji Apaji and Lakhamaji Apaji Nigade who had a quarrel with each other about the right over the watan. They approached the King and requested him to decide the dispute. The King issued an order to his officer of prant to enquire into the case and dispense justice with an aid of Gota. The Gotamajlis which was summoned in the temple of Shri Dev prepared the mahzar and was attended by Bhivaji Malhar hawaldar, Narahari Shivdev Majumdar and the Deshaks such as Yaraji Apaji Yeshwantrao, the Deshmukh, Tawaji Deshmukh, Sodu Naik, Sobaji Sonwani, Kaloji the mokadam of mauje Sangawi and Pargaon Gangaji, Gulab, Yadav Joshi, Ram Joshi, Shete Mahajan etc., while distributing the right over the

Deshkulkarni watan Vithoji Gorakhoji was mentioned in the mahzar as elder and hence the rights to the eldest person were granted to him. But in fact the father Bahiraji Apaji Nigade was the elder one who had gone to Chandi at the time of making of the division of the said watan. When he came back to the native place, he made a complaint to King Shivaji on Raigad against Vithoji Gurkhoji. After hearing of the complaint, the King issued an order to the Deshmukh to decide the case. The Deshmukh advised the plaintiff to go to the place namely Haranas in taluka Velvandkhore for the decision. Babaji Deshmukh, the government officer who presided over the meeting of the majlis, summoned the Gota at Haranas consisting of Harbhat, Purohit Joshi, Moreshwar Joshi, Shivabhat Joshi, Antaji Moredev, Deshkulkarni, Yes Patil, Khot of mauje Halwadi, Krishnaji Naik, Deshmukh, Lakhamoji Naik, and Yesaji Naik Deshmukh, Sonaji Naik Kakade, mokadam of mauje Baburdi. The mahzar speaks that Apaji Malaji Naik Nigode who made a complaint that out of the watan rights, Vithoji Gorkhoji Naik was enjoying one chavar of land and five hons as the rights to be enjoyed by the eldest person in the family. But he was enjoying these rights falsely. Because Apaji Malaji Naik Nigade was the elder person and Vithoji was the younger one. He made a petition to the King that the rights to elderness were to be granted to him. To this, Vithoji Naik replied that though his father was younger brother, after the death of his father, he held the responsibility of conducting the administration of the said watan. Hence, the rights of seniority granted to the eldest person were to be enjoyed by him. The members of the Gota who assembled in the temple of goddess of Shree for justice, gave verdict that the seniority rights were to be restored to Apaji Malaji Naik who was the eldest person in the family and Vithoji Gorakhaji had no claim over those rights. He was to be satisfied with other rights over the watan granted him by the Gota by way of division among the claimants. The persons who served as the witnesses to the decision pronounced by the Gota were Krishnaji Naik Silimkar, the Deshmukh of taluka Gunjmal Mawal, Raghoji Krishnaji Dohar Velisdar the Deshmukh of mauje Jogawadi of taluka Velvandkhore etc.[10]

Another dispute over the mokadami watan is notable here for the manner in which it was decided by the Gotamajlis. The Gotamajlis of pargana Indapur which prepared a mahzar on 8th August, 1639, was presided over by the Deshmukh namely Magaji Yemaji and was attended by Godaji mokadam of mauje Sevgaon, Lingoji the mokadam of mauje Jabu, Malaji Chaudaji, the mokadams of villages like Lakadi and Chikali, Kurbavikar of Dahigaon, Khandoji of Varkute etc. The dispute is related to the watan of mokadam of village Bori. Kheloji Bhosale had claimed over that mokadami watan of mauje Bori. But he was also demanding the horses using them as his right. The Kulkarni and Deshmukh were of the opinion that the said mokadami should be divided between Biroji mokadam of mauje Lasurane and the mokadam of Bori. Hence, a Mirasdar who also claimed over that watan made a complaint against them. Though in practice, Biroji had made an attempt for bringing more land under cultivation, much of the land in village remained barren. During this year Mirza had destroyed the crops and plundered animals. Therefore, the Gotamajlis decided to divide half of the mokadami watan of the village between Yeloji and Jabaji Wagmode and other half was given to Mau Biroji.[11] All the rights over the Pandhari and black land belonging to the village were to be enjoyed by both parties. The Gota also decided the complicated dispute regarding the boundaries of lands belonging to the villages of Kasba Supe and mauje Vadhane in Poona prant.[12] This dispute was once settled in 1526 by preparing a mahzar which was preserved by the men of Supe village. But it was too old to bring it into the practice. The members of the Gota examined the old document and found that same mahzar did not bear the signatures or signs of the witnesses such as Deshmukh, Deshak, Jawar diwan and the government clerks of the mahals who attended the meeting and were present at the time of the decision. Consequently, the mahzar was not considered as true. Therefore, the Gota of both villages consisting of the mokadams and other members fixed the boundaries of land and settled the dispute. Similarly another case of Sambhaji and Dharoji, disputed watan was decided by the Gota. Sambhaji and Dharoji two brothers were enjoying the watan of villages like Talbid and Wanji performing the duties jointly. But after their death, a quarrel between Shankaraji and Netaji began and in January 1662, it came up for the decision before the Gota which examined the previous records and tried the witnesses and finally gave decision that Shankaraji was to enjoy two parts of the watan and Dipaji and Netaji were to enjoy each one of the remaining two.[13]

The Gota also decided the seniority rights over the said watan. Accordingly, Shankaraji was to enjoy them first, then Dipaji and Netaji were to enjoy these rights one by one. Again the dispute over same mokadami watan of Tabid began between Sauji Mohite and Netaji Mohite in September 1663. The Gotasabha of the village consisting of officers, balutedars of Talbid, finally reached the decision that each of them was to enjoy half of the mokadami watan alongwith the right of seniority. But at the same time, the Gota did not allow Sauji to enjoy the Deshmukhi watan.[14] The Subhedar who presided over the meeting of the majlis dispensed justice with an aid of the Gota. The dispute regarding the Deshmukhi watan of Gunjanmawal arose between Bahuji Habaji Haibatrao and Balaji Rudraji. Dadaji Kondadev, who was the Subhedar of fort Kondana summoned the Gota consisted of Deshmukh Deshak and gave the decision by dividing the Deshmukhi watan equally among three persons who claimed over it. Accordingly, each of them was to enjoy one-third part of the watan and the seniority rights were to be enjoyed by Bahuji Haibatrao first then Habaji and Balaji were to enjoy them respectively.[15]

Another dispute about the Deshmukhi watan of taluka Gaud in Supe prant is worthy to be mentioned as it was decided by the village Gota or by the Juries of mauje Sirasgaon. The dispute arose between Shamraj Kate and Sambhaji Kate in 1656, over the said watan. Sambhaji Kate in 1656, over the said watan, appeared before Sambhaji Mohite, the officer of pargana and made a complaint against Shamraj Kate who did not enjoy the rights of Deshmukhi watan as was decided by earlier Gota. Hence, the officer of Thana summoned the meeting of the members of the Gota (who were called as Juries) of mauje Sirasgaon and gave the judgement with their consultation that village Sirasgaon be given to Shamraj and remaining villages of the mokasas were to be divided between two parties, out of which half of it was entrusted to Shamraj and Sambhaji Kate, the Deshmukhs of Supe pargana.[16]

On many occasions, the Rajmudra and the Sabha Naik also took the assistance of the Gotasabha in deciding the dispute over the watan. For example, when a dispute arose between Balaji Parasaram, Narso Somnath and Vitthal Ganesh Khade regarding the Kulkarni watan of Jejuri in 1677 A.D., the Gotasabha which was summoned was presided over by the Rajmudra. It was attended by the Sabha Naik and the mokadams of the village. It dispensed the justice by declaring the judgement that the said watan was to be equally divided among those brothers who demanded for it. Every one of them was to enjoy the equal rights over the Kulkarni watan.[17] When the King granted the mokadami watan to the person who sacrificed for the state, the mahzar prepared by the Gota declaring the rights of the patikli watan to the concerning person was necessary. For instance, Bakaji Farjand who performed hard work for the King, Shivaji granted him the patilki watan of village Khamgaon. He was to enjoy the rights and Inam like those of the patil of Mokhtsar. The King issued an order to the Subhedar of prant Mawal to summon the meeting of the Gota and the village balutas for preparing of the mahzar declaring that the said patil watan would be continued in the name of Bakaji.[18] Such mahzar was to be written by the Gota and handed over it to Bakaji Farjand. The Gotasabha at village level was attended not only by the Patil, the Deshmukh, Kulkarni but also by the Mahar Balutas. The Gotasabha met at mauje Pasine was summoned to decide the dispute over the Kulkarni watan arose between Sindbhat and Chandrabhat. Sindbhat had made a complaint to the Subhedar of prant Mawal against Chandrabhat who was creating the disturbance in enjoying of his rights over the said watan. The Subhedar asked the hawaldar abstain Chandrabhat from doing so. Sindbhat went to the Subha officer and brought the Khurdakhat from him for showing it to the village Gota. When the Gota asked the complainant and the defender to remain present before it for making of an enquiry of them, Chandrabhat could not remain present before Gota, which gave decision by continuing the said Kulkarni watan in the name of Sindbhat only.[19]

The members who attended the meeting of the Gota were the Patils of nine villages, the Deshmukh, Kulkarni and Mahar balutas of the villages etc. On some important occasions, when valuable issues were to be decided the Gotasabha was attended by prominent persons like King or the persons of royal family. Thus, for instance, the dispute arose in October 1652 A.D., between Dadaji Narasprabhu and Babaji Siwadev Sontake regarding the Deshkulkarni watan of Utroli in taluka Bhor. The meeting of the Gotasabha was held at Utroli under auspices of King Shivaji. The issue that was brought before the Gotasabha decided that the watan was to be equally divided between two persons namely Dadaji Narasprabhu and Babaji Sontake. But the latter wrote a false statement on the mahzar and showed that the said watan belonged to him only. After going through the mahzar, and examining it carefully by the members of the Gota who took the Ajit-patra from the defaulter, the document proved to be false.[20] Consequently the claims of Babaji Sontake over the said watan also proved to be false. Sometimes, the

Gotasabha was presided over by the government officials (Rajmudra) such as Chief Officer of Mahal and well learned men etc. The Hazir Majlis of mauje Supe Khurd was summoned in October 1658 and Ramaji Balal, Yado Narayan Sabhasad were the mahal officer and learned person respectively under whose auspices the meeting of Gotasabha was held. The plaintiff namely Khandoji Garud made a complaint to King Shivaji against Mali Jagtap regarding the mokadami watan of the village. He was enjoying the rights of the said watan since longer period, but he had to leave the village and had to migrate to Bijapur prant. But when he left the village, he asked Mali Jagtap to look after the watan and to conduct the administration of mokadami watan of Supe. But after some days, Mali Jagtap who claimed over the village watan, began to quarrel with the plaintiff. So the King issued an order to the Gotasabha of Supe to decide the dispute. Besides the prominent persons or the state officials, following is the list of the names of other members of Gota who were also present at the time of dispensing the justice to the parties.

Rajmudra

Rajshri Ramaji Balal (Mahal, Saswad)	Yado Narayan, Sabhasad

The meeting of Gota was attended by the watandars like Samaraj Kate Deshmukh, Gomadev Deshkulkarni, the Naikwadi and the Deshaks such as Apaji Tilekar Mokadam of mauje Khalad, Kondaji Akarasa, mokadam of mauje Gujawadi, Trimbakaji Darkar, Mokadam of Abale Babaji Jagtap, Tanaji Chaugula, Kanhoji Chaudhari mokadam of mauje Khore, Mankoji Kamatha Patil of Chambali etc. The village balutedars of Maar, Pariche etc., were also present at the meeting.[21] The Gota took the decision that the case should be examined carefully and the balutas of Bhowargaon were to be consulted for finding out the truth. The record seems to be silent as to what further and final decision was given by the Gota which took the advice of the balutas for declaring the judgement on the dispute.[22] The Mahaldar, the Chief Officer of Thana, who discharged other administrative functions, also enjoyed the judicial powers. Thus, when a dispute arose between Kedaraji Zabira Patel, Dogarsoni and Tukoji Dhangar, regarding the Patil watan of mauje Ped in mamle Murtazabad, the case was brought before the Mahaldar of thana Purnur Mahamadpur for decision. The majlis consisting of Dabir, Yemaji Naryan Majumdar, the mahal officers like Daffardar, Yel Naik, Naikwadi, and Sakhawatkhan Alishan mahaldar etc., and village residents. The majlis was presided over by Babaji Hasan mahaldar of thana Purnur Mahamadpur and it prepared the mahzar by taking witnesses of village residents such as Apaji Kulkarni, Annaji Chaugala, Baloji Khot etc., who supported the cause of Tukoji Dhangar, by making the statements that they alongwith Dhangar family were enjoying the rights over the patil watan since the period of five generations. The members of majlis with the assistance of Sarkhel mamalik and Sabha Naik gave verdict jointly in favour of Tukoji Dhangar and the patil watan was conferred on him. The claims of Kedaraji Zabira Dogarsoni over the rights of watan declared to be false. The hawaldar Nematkhan who prepared the Katabas of the parties, sent them to Sakhawatkhan the Mahaldar for deciding the case. The Sarkhel thus decided the dispute in favour of Tukoji Dhangar.[23] A case between Kheloji and Viroji in which both parties claimed over the mokadami watan of mauje Bori. The suit was brought before the Gota of the village, which decided the case by examining the evidences presented before it. The Gota declared the judgement that all the black and pandhari land of the village watan should be divided between those two persons. The half of the watan was to be divided between Yeloji and Jabaji Waghmode, the sons of Kheloji and another half was to be restored to Viroji.[24]

Another dispute regarding mokadami watan of mauje Chikhalgaon in tarf Rohidkhore arose between two brothers namely Vagoji Dhonda Patil and Hiroji Dhonda Patil. Vagoji Dhonda was the elder brother of Hiroji who forcibly took the watan from the complainant and paid twelve hundred hons as the rasad to the government and got a farman showing the watan in his name. It is further mentioned in the plaint that Hiroji had produced false documents before the government officer. To this, Hiroji had replied that his elder brother namely Vagoji was sent to the government to deposit the amount against the permission to be granted to him for conducting the mokadami watan of Chikhalgaon. Being the elder son of the father, he claimed his seniority rights over the watan. But in fact, Hiroji Patil looked after the administration of said watan and he had taken pains to bring more land of village under cultivation. Hiroji demanded that the Yejijkhat a letter showing all the rights over the watan to be given up by his elder brother, would be written and taken from Vagoji. He also willingly agreed before the Gota to cede half of the Inam to his elder brother.[25] As the record is incomplete, it does not throw much light on further decision announced by the village Gota. The Gotasabha at village level met at mauje Ravet in Poona pargana was presided over by the Subhedar and was attended by the mokadams of villages like Khadakwasale, Anjangaon, the Kulkarni and Chaugula of village Loni Kalabhor. It was attended by Lessor watandars such as Patils, Kulkarni and Kunbis, balutas etc. The meeting of the Gotasabha was called to decide the dispute arose between Malajee Bhoita and Bhiloji Malajee regarding the Patilki watan. The Gota Majlis of mauje Ravet examined the evidences and declared the judgement in favour of Bhilojee.[26]

Similarly, Gotasabha was also attended by the watandars at higher level like the Deshmukhs. For instance, in 1638 A.D., the Gotasabha[27] presided over by Dadaji Kondadev, met to decide the dispute regarding the Deshmukhi watan and was attended by the Deshmukhs of Khedebare and Kanadkhore, Mosekhore, Gunjanmawal.

Other members who also remained present were the Deshaks, Kulkarnis and Mokadams etc. The word "Deshak" seems to have applied to village watandars like mokadams, Khasnis, Kulkarni etc. The head of the Deshak was the Deshmukh.[28]

REFERENCES AND FOOTNOTES

1. MIS XVI, Letter No. 22
2. SCS II, Letter No. 281
3. Ibid, II, Letter No. 98
4. Ibid, II, P. 126
5. Ibid, VIII, Letter No. 70
6. Ibid, VIII, Letter No. 71, P. 79
7. Ibid, VIII, Letter No. 70
8. Purandare Daftar, Part III, Letter No. 154
9. MIS, XX, Letter No. 54
10. Ibid, XX, PP. 93-94
11. SCS III, Letter No. 632
12. SPSS I, Letter No. 100
13. SPSS I, Letter Nos. 869 and 954
14. Ibid, I, Letter Nos, 954 and 955
15. Ibid, I, Letter No. 432
16. Records of Shivaji period, Letter No. 19
17. SCS 7, Letter No. 58
18. SCS II, Letter No. 277
19. Ibid II, Letter No. 110
20. SPSS I, Letter Nos. 623 and 626
21. SCS, III, Letter No. 640
22. Ibid, III, P. 233
23. Ibid, III, Letter No. 638
24. SPSS, Letter No. 2469
25. Ibid, III, Letter Nos. 2490 and 2491
26. MIS, XVIII, Letter No. 7
27. Ibid XVII, Letter No. 7
28. Gune V.T., JSM, P. 167

5

Provincial Administration of Civil and Criminal Justice

Administrative Divisions of Kingdom

The territory of Maharashtra under the rule of Chhatrapati Shivaji was known as Swaraj which comprised the region extending from Salher in Baglan, the northern boundary of his state, to Kopal in the south. The northern region of his Kingdom comprised Kalyan-Bhiwandi, Jawahar etc. The Thalghat or the southern area of his country included Dabhol, Rajapur, Phonda and the Varghat included the land extending from Poona to Kopal. His dominion thus included only the Salher territory in North Talghat region and the country of Desh above the ghat in South. The whole Kingdom under Shivaji was partitioned into three divisions. For the administrative purpose, the area of Kalyan-Bhiwandi, Varghat and Konkan was kept under the supervision of Peshwa Moropant. The Lohagad, Junner and Boramawal etc., were also controlled by the Peshwa. The region extending from Cheul, Dabhol, Rajapur, Kudar Bande to Phonda and Kopal was supervised by Annaji Datto. The land extending from Wai to Kopal Tungabhadra was kept under the supervision of Annaji Suranavis.[1] In short, every division of his Kingdom was kept under the control of King's agents like Peshwa, Chitnis and the minister.[1a] The Kingdom was divided in the Subhas. The

Subha was the largest territorial unit in the state. The head of the Subha was known as Subhedar. It appears that when the Subha was more than one or two units or of large size, the head of it was known as Sarsubhedar.[1b]

Subhedar (An Officer of Subha Majlis)

The Subhedar or Sarsubhedar the head of the Subha possessed the power of dispensing justice and also executed the decision. He was the Chief Police Officer of the Subha.[1c] The system of separation of judiciary from the executive did not prevail in Shivaji's Kingdom. The Subhedar who was to look after the working of Subha Majlis also presided over it.[2] He heard the complaints of the people and worked as a judge to decide the suits came up to him. Mostly he referred the criminal cases to the King. The orders issued to the authorities of prants from time to time by King Shivaji reveal that the Subhedar held the responsibility of general supervision over the civil and criminal justice in the territory under his jurisdiction. The Deshmukh of pargana sent the civil cases to the Subhedar for the decision. Sometimes, the Subhedar also sent the civil cases to the Deshmukh who with the help of the Gota majlis of pargana investigated the matter or tried those suits. The Subhedar was one of the members of the majlis which prepared the mahzar declaring of the sale and purchase of the watan. He issued an order to the majlis to prepare such mahzars which pronounced the sale of Inam land and handed over them to the concerning persons involved in the need of sale and purchase land.[3] The Subhedar was the highest officer in the Subha and the representative of King Shivaji. He was next to the King in provincial administration of justice. Being Chief Official and executive head of Subha, he had to administer justice in province as one of his duties. He had to decide the civil cases of disputed watans under his jurisdiction.[4] Visaji Ballal, the Subhedar of prant Poona was instructed by Shivaji to administer justice to Pantaji Gopinath Bokil who claimed over the rights of Deshkulkarni watan of Supe and Baramati parganas. In cases of disputes regarding the claims over the watans, the Subhedar was called upon to give his judgement with the help of Gota. By taking the witnesses of the Deshakas for the decision, he prepared the document of judgement and sent it to King Shivaji. Ragho Ballal, the Subhedar, who presided over the Hazir Majlis of peth Narayanpur fort Purandar met on 10th September 1676 A.D., heard the complaint made by Das Patil Malwadkar of mauje Jejuri regarding the patil watan against Suryaji Malwadkar. The Subhedar issued a letter to Gholap, the hawaldar of fort Purandar, Ganaji Madgal the Sarhawaldar of mamle to enquire into the case. He asked them to give verdict by summoning the meeting of the Gota consisting of the mokadams, balutas and deity worshippers of Jejuri who served as the witnesses to the decision of the Gota.[5]

Similar dispute regarding the village mokadami of mauje Mekhali was brought by two persons before the Subhedar of fort and mahal Kondana. The Subhedar gave an order to the Deshmukh of the pargana to dispense justice with the help of the Gota.[6] It was his duty to issue the documents like Khurdakhat to the person approaching the Majlis for the decision of the watan. Thus, as per the order of King Shivaji issued in 1676 A.D., Mahadaji Shamraj, the Subhedar of Mawale prant, had to prepare the documents of Sarpatilkiwatan called as Khurdakhat and hand over it to Suryaji Patil, the mokadam of mauje Sivare in taluka Khedebare.[7]

Similar dispute regarding the Kulkarni watan of mauje Chikhali was settled in 1672 by Ragho Ballal Atre, the Subhedar of Sararkar Junnar.[8] Another Subhedar namely Raje Palkar Sarnobat[9] heard the complaint about patil watan made by Mahadaji Randive against Godaji Patil Panchputa. The Subhedar referred the case to the Gota for deciding the dispute. This chief officer of Subha also tried the dispute about money. Thus, Krishnaji Bhaskar, the Subhedar of Mahal, got the complaint from the Deshkulkarni against Gujarati Haikaji Jedha who borrowed sixty takas from the complainant but did not repay it in stipulated time. Hence, the Subhedar asked the hawaldar namely Bahiraji Wagh to enquire into the matter and issue the final instruction to the debtor to return the amount to the creditor.[10] Thus it shows that the hawaldar of tarf was under direct supervision of Subhedar. The officer of the Subha issued him instructions for investigating into the nature of offences brought before him by the complainants. The Subhedars such as Siddhi Hilal of Thane, Ragho Mahadev of Supe and others were empowered to issue the orders to the Deshpandes of the pargana to examine the documents or Sanads about rights and perquisites of the watan and issue them permission to look after their watans.[10]

While conducting the judicial duties or deciding the disputed cases of watan, the Subhedar had to take the assistance of the Deshmukh of pargana by issuing him a letter of instructions for taking a written agreement about the final decision (known as Rajinama) from both the parties by the officer. For instance, in 1658 A.D., Konher Ranganath Sarsubhedar of prant Karhad sent a letter to Pilava Deshmukhin of Wai pargana regarding the dispute of the watan of Dhomthadi between Shankar Joshi of Wai and Apadev Bhat Adakar. The Sarsubhedar instructed the Deshmukhin to take the Rajinama from the litigants sent to her by him. He also asked her to ascertain the truth with the help of majlis and send the report about the decision to the Government.[12] In deciding the disputes, he also took the help of the hawaldar of the tarf to investigate into the judicial matter. Thus, in May 1656 A.D., Abaji Mahadev, the Sarsubhedar of Subha Kalyan-Bhiwandi wrote a letter to Ragho Anant, the hawaldar of the Deshkulkarni who committted the crime by misappropriating the revenue amount. The hawaldar was instructed by the Subhedar to enquire into his practice of not keeping the accounts in detail which afforded an opportunity for fraud to the revenue officer.[13] The Subhedar possessed the power to supervise over the administration of civil justice and gave the sanction to the Patilkiwatan granted by the King to various persons. For instance, the Patilkiwatan in Mawal taluka purchased from Dadaji Kondadev Deshmukh belonged to the State. Then the same Patil watan was granted by King to Mankoji Gaikwad. But the King issued a letter to Mahadaji Samaraj, the Subhedar of prant to continue the said watan in the name of Mankoji Gaikwad.[14]

Thus, it appears that the approval of the Subhedar with his seal on the document of watan transaction was considered as necessary for its legal validity. The Subhedar was to examine the documents regarding the Inam lands granted by the King to various men and then allowed to continue the Inams in their names. Thus, in 1670 A.D., Mahadaji Govind, the Subhedar of Poona prant, wanted to examine the document regarding the Inam land granted to Nilkantrao[15] by King Shivji and therefore, the officer demanded the same document from him. On representation of written document by Nilkantrao from Shivaji, the Subhedar allowed to continue the Inam land in his name. Thus, with the approval of the Subhedar, the Inam land in the name of Inam holder was to be continued and the Inam land could finally become as valid.

The Subhedar had to supervise the prisoners kept in the Adabkhana. The prisoners could be released from the confinement on the recommendation of the Subhedar. For instance, Shree Sindgonda Desai and Murarirao Trimal Deshkulkarni of Hukeri pargana who had committed crime, were imprisoned on the fort of Raigad. Hiroji Indalkar, the Subhedar of the fort made a request to King Shivaji to dispose of the prisoners who were in prison since long time. It appears that the King gave respect to the request of the Subhedar and released the prisoners from prison.[16] The King also assigned the responsibility of conducting the Deshkulkarni watan in prant Ajire to Murarirao, in 1679 A.D.[17]

The Subhedar also supervised the cases of land revenue. He could decide the disputed cases involving the Inam lands and their revenues too. In order to continue the Inam land to the Inam holders, on the recommendation of the King, the Subhedar could issue the sanads by granting such lands in the name of those persons.[18] He also supervised the judiciary function of the hawaldar. Thus, Mahadaji Samraj, the Subhedar of Mawal prant had to control over the work of hawaldar of tarf namely Mahadaji Narasprabhu. When a dispute over Kulkarni watan of mauje Ahire was heard by the Subhedar, he issued an instruction to the hawaldar. The latter was instructed that though Sindhbhat Thakur brought the "Khurdakhat" and showed it to the hawaldar, the Subhedar asked him to abstain the person from bringing obstacles in the enjoyment of Janaki's rights over the said watan.[19] It was the duty of the Subhedar to transfer the watan in the name of another person who bought it from an earlier watandar. In March 1672, Vitthal Piladeu, the Subhedar of Mawal prant was asked by the King to transfer the Kulkarni and Jyotisi watan of mauje Elake of pargana Sirwal in the name of Yamaji Rangnath Bokil who purchased it from another person. The Deshaks were to prepare the mahzar showing the claims of the purchaser over the watan that was transferred to his name.[20]

The Subhedar was authorised to collect some amount as fee to be covered by the parties involved in the dispute. Dadaji Kondadev the Subhedar of Poona prant decided the dispute between Ratnoji and Parinchkar with the help of the Gota and collected twenty-two hons from Krishnaji who paid the amount on behalf of Ratnoji.[21] The Subhedar could possess the power to grant new Inam land to the person who got it in exchange of an earlier Inam. Thus, Babuji Zunzar Rau, the Deshmukh of Khandkhore was directed by the Subhedar of Kondana to grant the Inam at Dapoda to Babaji in exchange of his earlier Inam at Anturli.[22]

Deshmukh (An Officer of Pargana Majlis)

The chief officials attached with the pargana Gotamajlis were the Deshmukh and the Deshpande. The Deshmukh of pargana not only supervised the revenue affairs but also looked after the judicial cases. He usually summoned the Gotamajlis of pargana and presided over its meeting held to give verdicts on civil disputes.[23]

The Deshmukh had jurisdiction over civil as well as criminal disputes in pargana. He had to supervise the disputes of land revenue and other judicial complaints lodged with the mokadams in the pargana. The Deshmukh under whose supervision the Gotamajlis of pargana prepared the mahzar, acted as the witness to the judgement pronounced by the majlis.[24] It was his duty to collect the government dues from the Mutalik.[25] He was to watch the proceedings of the pargana majlis and send the report about the dispute to the King.[26] It was the duty of the Deshmukh to prepare the document like "Rokha" when the case was sent for trial to other locality called as "thal" for deciding the suit. For instance, the dispute over the Deshkulkarni watan of Khedebare was to be decided by the Deshmukh. The plaintiff made a request to King Shivaji to issue an order to the Deshmukh of pargana Khedebare to prepare the document known as Rokha, which was necessary for sending the case to other place for decision. On the request of the complainant King Shivaji asked the Deshmukh officer to prepare the document in the names of Chimanaji Bapuji and Sakhoji Bhikaji who were involved in the case.

The Deshmukh was to take the security from the person who during the period of his absence desired to go to another place for decision.[27] The same person was to give the name of his witness to the Deshmukh.[28] But if the litigant refused to go to another place for the judgement, the Deshmukh was to send the report about the willingness of the person to King Shivaji.[29] On the occasion of taking the evidence of Gohi, the Deshmukh was to act as Gohi. For instance, when a dispute regarding the rights of seniority over the watan arose, Buwai Awa, the Deshmukh of the pargana, acted as the Gohi.[30] It is to be noted that the mahzar prepared by the Gora pargana could become valid when it was signed by the Deshmukh, the Chairman of the Sabha. Thus, the mahzar prepared by the Sabha and possessed by Keshavpant not only contained the names of the witnesses but also the signature of the pargana officer.[31] The Deshmukh was to act as a judge while dividing the rights of the Deshkulkarni watan between the litigants. A Deshmukh of pargana Shirwal decided the dispute regarding the Kulkarni watan of said pargana between Kanhopant and Purushottampant in presence of the Shete of the kasba.[32] The main duty of the Deshmukh was to receive the complaints from the plaintiff and take the statements (takarira) regarding the dispute from him.[33] And after going through the Khurdakhat, he had to give his judgement on the suits. The Khurdakhat written by the government officer and brought before the Deshmukh, was necessary for the transfer of the Inam land[34] and for deciding the case. But it appears that the Deshmukh was to give the verdict on watan dispute not only by examining the Khurdakhat, but also by taking the witnesses of village residents. The Deshmukh officer of Akole pargana was strictly warned by the King to decide the dispute regarding the Deshpande watan between Tubaji Gangadhar Deshpande and Dhondo Govind, not by consulting only the Khurdakhat, but by summoning the village men before him to give their witnesses.[35] The King also gave him power to decide the cases involving the rights over the watan.[36] While acting as a Judge, the Deshmukh was to perform following works in administering the justice to the people. It was he who was to tell the Karina[37] or (story of dispute) or written statements given by the plaintiff before the members of the Hazir Majlis when summoned for deciding the case. In deciding the dispute of mokadami watan, he was to ascertain the truth regarding the rights over the watan and acted as one of the witnesses.[38] When a mokadam of the village lost his documents regarding the watan, he could apply to the Deshmukh of the pargana to prepare such documents claiming his rights over the watan. For instance, Wet Patil, Agari Patil, the grandsons of Mahadu Patil, the mokadam of mauje Kusubale came up to Cheul pargana and made a request to the Deshmukh Officer that his forefather was enjoying the mokadami watan of said village. But the documents concerning that watan were lost due to the calamity like flood. But by tradition the same watan was enjoyed by the members of his family. He, therefore, made a request to the Deshmukh of Cheul pargana to prepare a mahzar claiming his rights over the Mokadami.[39] Finally, the Deshmukh who summoned other witnesses to testify the claims of the person over the Mokadami watan, prepared the mahzar with the help of Deshkulkarni revealing his rights over the said watan duly attested by a number of mokadams of the villages in the pargana and gave the Jabata to the concerned person.[40] In deciding the case of Kulkarni watan, the Deshmukh alongwith other officers such as Shete-Mahajan and the Deshaks also called the members of litigant's village as Gohidars for taking their witnesses. All those witnesses (gohidars) were to take the oath before the Deshmukh, the Government officer, for speaking the truth about the issues involved in the dispute.[41] While administering the justice, the practice of performing an ordeal by means of hot piece of metal was observed before the Deshmukh who was to remain present there at the time of the performance of an ordeal. In order to ascertain the truth regarding the Kulkarni Watan of pargana Supe, the person namely Khade had to perform an ordeal before the Deshmukh and Deshkularni of Saswad.[42] In finding the truth about the criminal cases like killing of the persons, the Deshmukh played an important role as a government officer of judiciary. For instance, when Apaji Deshmukh was murdered by Ramoji who gave him poison, the persons like Jagdevrao,

Rohidekar, Purandarkar etc., were summoned by Malharaji Deshmukh of the mahal for making their enquiry of the mahal for finding out the truth about the murder of Apaji Farjand Deshmukh.[43] One of the judicial duties of the Deshmukh was to prepare the document called as Lakota that was necessary for performing of an ordeal. After preparing it, he was to give it to the person who desired to prove the truth of his statement by means of an ordeal.[44]

Hawaldar, an Officer of Mahal or Thana

The Hazir Majlasi of Thana pargana was presided over by the Government Officer like Hawaldar.[45] He could decide the boundary dispute between two villages.[46] The hawaldar was authorised to ask the faujdar of the locality to decide the dispute between two communities with the help of Brahmasabha. It was the duty of the hawaldar to send the report about the judgement declared by the Majlis to the King.[47]

Ramaji Balal, the hawaldar of Taluka Karhepathar Saswad received an order from the King to decide the dispute regarding the Mokadami Watan with the help of Gota. He summoned the Hazir Majlis with the assistance of Sabha Naiki. He also issued an order to the Gota and held its meeting to decide the Mokadami Watan.[48] When the dispute was brought before the chief officer of pargana Majlis, the hawaldar had to perform the following important judicial functions. In case of dispute, in his jurisdiction of market place, it was the duty of the hawaldar to remain present at the time of preparing of Karina.[49] His presence was necessary when the statements of litigants were taken by the other pargana officer. The hawaldar was held as a responsible officer when the litigant desired that his case should be decided by trial of an ordeal. The hawaldar was one of those government officers such as the Deshmukh, the Naikwadi, the mokadam Shete-Mahajan etc., who examined the Yejijkhat brought by the defendant for showing to them.

After going through the document they prepared the mahzar jointly and offered it to the person.[50] If the plaintiff desired to perform an ordeal at another place, it became the duty of the hawaldar of Thana to prepare the documents called as Thalpatra and Jayapatra (a letter issued to successful litigant) and hand over it to the concerning person.[51]

The hawaldar was empowered to allow to conduct the watan to the person who showed him the Khurdkhat. For instance, Haibatkhan the hawalder of Supe pargana granted the Kulkarni and Joshi watan of the villages like Kolvihire and Navili to Khadiya[52] who showed him the Khurdkhat that was necessary to grant the permission to conduct the watan to the watan holders. Sometimes, the plaintiff could ascertain the truth by undertaking the ordeal successfully and got the Jayapatra from the government officer of the place. Then the defendant could make a complaint to the hawaldar of Thana regarding the false ordeal which was performed by opposite party. For instance, with a view of finding out the truth, Belsare had performed ordeal successfully and his claims over Kulkarni and Jotish watan in Supe pargana were declared to be true by the Government officer. But Parasbhat, Vithalbhat Khade who were defendants, appeared before the hawaldar of mahal during the reign of Malik Ambar and he made a complaint against Belsare that an ordeal performed by him was unsuccessful and his claims over the said watan proved to be false. He also made a request to the officer to decide the dispute by examining all the evidences carefully.[53] The hawaldar was to look after the administration of prison also. He had to keep the record of the offenders confined in prison and also the details about the offences committed by them.

In fact the nature of the work of hawaldar was certainly that of a police officer also. Madhavaji Krishna, the hawaldar issued an order to Kondaji Patel and brought him before the highest authority for making an enquiry as to why he failed in bringing more land in pargana of Wai under cultivation. The hawaldar gave him warning that even if he failed so again, then the Patel was to give up his rights over the watan.[54] It was also a part of duty of a hawaldar to see that no mokadam should create obstacles in enjoying the rights of Kulkarni watan by any man conducting the duty of the village accountant. The hawaldar of Poona pargana issued the warning to the Mokadam of Parvati who abstained Vinayakbhat Thakar from enjoying his rights over the Kulkarni watan of the villages of Narhe and Parvati.[55] If the mokadam again brought obstacle in conducting of business of Kulkarni, then it was the hawaldar who could bring the Mokadam before the King or gave punishment to the village Patil.[56] The hawaldar was to maintain peace and order in territory under his jurisdiction. King Shivaji issued an order to Mukund Dhondadev, the hawaldar of Khedebare taluka to punish Chandkhan the Mokadam of kasba Khedebare who violated the peace and order by making disturbances.[57] It was his duty to keep the offender in prison and put iron rings among his feet. The hawaldar of Supe pargana namely Sambhaji Mohite imprisoned Timaji Khanderao for a period of three months and beat him daily. The hawaldar also put iron rings in his feet during the period of his confinement.[58] He was required to collect the amount decided by the majlis for the settlement of the dispute from the parties involved in it. For instance, Siwaji Kito, the Hawaldar of Poona pargana instructed Timaji Khanderao, the Kulkarni of mauje Kolhale to pay seventy-five hons to Visaji and Ramaji Uda who in return instead of cash, got a horse costing seventy-five hons from the Kulkarni.[59]

The hawaldar was to see that the debtor should repay the amount of loan to the creditor in due course. Bahiraji Prabhu, the hawaldar of Rohidkhore was instructed by the Subhedar of mahal to bring pressure upon Naikaji Jedha to repay the sixty takas borrowed by him from the Deshkulkarni namely Mahadaji Ram. The hawaldar was to see, when he received the complaint from the creditor, that the capital amount should be returned to the money lender by the borrower shortly. The defaulter if failed in refunding the loan to the banker, the hawaldar offered him punishment.[60] The litigant if proved as false or lost the case, he was to give in writing the Ajitkhat (a letter to be issued to unsuccessful candidate) before the hawaldar. For instance, Thanji Krishnaji Dimala of mauje Kalyan gave in writing the Ajitkhat before the hawaldar of fort Kondana to the successful person namely Bhikaji Dimala of mauje Siwar that his rights over the mokadami watan were false and he was not concerned with the mokadami watan of said village.[61] Such Ajitkhat was attested with the signatures of the Deshmukh and other mokadams of the pargana.[62] Thus, the various duties described above and also performed by the hawaldar of mahal give us an idea of the scope of his judicial activities.

The Mokadam – An Officer of Village Gotasabha

We find that the Mokadam in village performed duties of the police as well as civil duties. As a head of the village, the mokadam had the general supervision of village administration. On the judicial side, he was incharge of civil and criminal justice of the village. The mokadam acted as the Chairman of the village Gotasabha consisting of the inhabitants of village, the balutas and uparis etc.[63] Before performing the Rava ordeal the litigant had to inform the mokadam first about it.[64] After the completion of an ordeal, the litigant had to show his hands or palms to the mokadam, the chief of the Gotasabha as to let him know whether he performed an ordeal successfully or not.[65]

He also remained present when the mahzar about the dispute was prepared and it was necessary for the mokadam to put his signature on the mahzar. In revenue affairs he was to work under the supervision of the Deshmukh of the pargana.[66] The mokadam was to preside over the meeting of the Hazir Majlis Deshak which heard the complaint about the Mokadami watan of village. In this work the mokadam had to get the assistance of the village Gota to decide the dispute. One of the parties involved in the dispute was to give in writing the Yejitkhat (a letter of sacrifice of the right over the Watan) before the Chief of the Gota Sabha.[67] He also acted as one of the witnesses to the decision taken by the Gota over dispute.[68] He was empowered to give justice on the boundary dispute between two villages. For instance, Ramaji Bapuji, the mokadam of mauje Malshiras was to decide the boundary dispute between the villages like Tekawadi and Pisarawe in prant of Poona. The highest authority used to issue an order to Mokadam to decide the case with the help of an ordeal to be performed before the deity of Shri Vateshwar at Saswad.[69]

Chaugula

The judicial duties of the Chaugula were included such as remaining present at the time of preparing of the mahzar. He was to put his sign on it.[70] He also acted as the witness to the decision of the Hazir Majlis.

Majumdar

The majumdar was to remain present at the time of preparing of the Mahzar[71] on which his signature was necessary.[72] He also acted as one of the witnesses to the decision taken by the Hazir Majlis on dispute.[73]

Mahaldar

Mahaldar was to work under the supervision of hawaldar. He was to send the report to the King about the imprisoned persons. The plaintiff was to appear before the Mahaldar for making the complaint to him.[74] It was hawaldar who brought the litigants before the officer of the Majlis for giving the statements about the disputes.[75]

Officials' Conduct in Judicial Administration

In the rule of Shivaji, the capability, sincerity and honesty of the officials depended upon king's vigilance and his abilities to control the administrative machinery. King Shivaji governed his kingdom through his officials. He was very careful all the time to see that the officers carried out his orders and powers vested in administrative heads and their machinery should not be abused. All the officers were subject to the transfer from one locality to another. Sometimes, the transfer of the officers was made on account of serious fault committed by them. Such officers were liable to be punished. Though the chief aim of the king was to defend his kingdom by organizing the military strength, he was equally interested in collection of land revenue and also in the functions of the judiciary. The officers such as Subhedar, the Deshmukhs, the hawaldars, Mokadams etc., working in the judiciary were also assigned revenue and other administrative duties. Thus, the judiciary was not treated as an independent or separate institute in Shivaji's kingdom.

The king who possessed the power to appoint the officials or promote them, also punished the defaulters.

The conduct of the officials was subject to the king's control and vigilance. Many times, when the litigants were not satisfied with the evidences to be presented before the judicial authority for finding out the truth, then the emphasis was laid on trial by an ordeal.[76] King Shivaji and the council of his ministers at the centre were controlling forces over the Government machinery conducting the whole administration of justice of the State. Shivaji concentrated his attention exclusively upon maintaining the judicial administration in considerable high state of efficiency and honesty. Even rare cases of the administrative officials committing mal-practices like bribery and showing leniency towards criminals were treated roughly by the king. It cannot be denied that the method of committing bribery by men for judicial purpose was totally absent in kingdom of Shivaji. A few persons could secure the assistance of the judicial officials by offering them bribe for declaring the judgement in favour of them. An example of the practice of bribery observed by Sambhaji Mohite, the hawaldar of pargana, is a good example to illustrate the point. King Shivaji seems to have made very serious attempts to check such kind of practice by offering service punishments to those officials as in the case of Sambhaji Mohite, the hawaldar of Supe, the bribe in form of hons taken by him from the litigants to decide the case in his favour, highly annoyed by King Shivaji. The king finally dismissed him from his office and watan was confiscated and was sent into the prison. A similar severe attitude was naturally shown by King Shivaji towards the crime of embezzlement. Because such offence was related directly to king's treasury. The cases those we find in contemporary records about the accounts of bribery or corruption practised by Sate officials are negligible as compared with the number of cases of mal-practics of present times. The individual gains and short-sightedness of the officers mostly attracted them towards those dangerous practices which caused king's impartial judicial administration to suffer on certain level.

REFERENCES AND FOOTNOTES

1. Sabhasad Bakhar, PP. 94, 95, also see Sarkar J.N., Shivaji and his Times, P. 340
1a. SPSS, Letter Nos. 1671 and 1672, 1724
1b. Gune V.T., Op cit, P. 28
1c. Gune V.T., Op cit, P. 116
2. SCS, I, Letter Nos. 26 and 27
3. SCS, III, PP. 54-55
4. Ibid, VIII, Letter No. 57
5. Ibid, 7, Letter No. 57, P. 96
6. Ibid, 7, Letter No. 32
7. Ibid, III, Letter No. 628
8. SPSS, II, Letter No. 1482
9. SCS, I, Letter No. 49
10. Ibid, I, Letter No. 52
11. Ibid, 7, Letter No. 47
12. MIS, XX, Letter No. 176, P. 240
13. Purandare Daftar, Part III, Letter No. 152, P. 144
14. SCS 7, Letter No. 56
15. Ibid, I, Letter No. 53

16. SCS, VIII, Letter No. 12
17. Ibid, VIII, Letter No. 13
18. Ibid, VIII, Letter No. 59
19. Ibid, VIII, Letter No.109
20. SPSS, III, Letter No. 2735
21. Ibid, I, Letter No. 457
22. Ibid, I, Letter No. 507
23. MIS XV, Letter No. 430
24. SPSS, III, Letter No. 2424
25. Ibid, III, Letter No. 2424
26. SCS III, Letter Nos. 459 and 460
27. Purandare Daftar, Part III, P. 134
28. Ibid, Part III, P. 134
29. Ibid.
30. Ibid, P. 137
31. Ibid, P. 142
32. SCS I, P. 94
33. SPSS III, Letter No. 2462
34. Ibid, III, Letter No. 2520
35. Ibid, III, Letter No. 2654
36. Ibid, III, Letter No. 2657
37. SCS 7, Letter No. 31, P. 50
38. Ibid.
39. SCS 7, Letter No. 60
40. Ibid, P. 101
41. SCS I, P. 15
42. SCS 7, Letter No. 21, P. 30
43. SCS I, Letter No. 25, P. 46
44. SCS I, P.10
45. Ibid I, Letter No. 21, P. 33
46. SPSS I, Letter No. 216
47. Ibid, II, Letter No. 714
48. SCS II, Letter No. 98.
49. Purandare Daftar, Part III, P. 130
50. SCS 7, P. 28
51. Ibid
52. Ibid, P. 29
53. SCS 7, P. 30
54. SCS VIII P. 75

55. Ibid, I, Letter No. 30
56. Ibid, P. 53
57. Ibid, 7, Letter No. 55, P. 92
58. Ibid, 7, Letter No. 44, P. 65
59. Ibid, 7, Letter No. 45, P. 74
60. Ibid, I, Letter No. 52
61. Ibid, III, Letter No. 625
62. Ibid, P. 209
63. Ibid, III, Letter No. 567
64. Ibid, I, Letter No. 22, P. 39
65. Ibid, I, P. 39
66. Ibid, III, Letter No. 5777, P.181
67. SPSS, III, Letter Nos. 2490 and 2491
68. SCS, III, Letter No. 577
69. Spss, I, Letter No. 132
70. SCS, I, P. 19
71. Ibid, I, P. 31
72. Ibid, I, P. 31
73. Ibid, III, Letter No. 638
74. Ibid, III, P. 225
75. Ibid III, P. 222
76. Ibid, I, Letter No. 22, SCS, V, Letter No. 831, SCS VIII, Letter No. 21

6

Judicial Procedure, Offence and Penalty

Judicial procedure as was followed by the judicial officers of Shivaji and found in our records may be described into following stages :

(i) Receiving plaint from Agrawadi
(ii) Receiving statements of defendant (pashchimvadi)
(iii) Evidence
(iv) Judicial verdict

Receiving Statements from Agrawadi and Paschimwadi

From the documents regarding the judicial decisions known as Mahzar, it appears that the litigant could appear before king or government officers such as Subheder of prant, Deshmukh of pargana, the hawaldar of mahal or mokadam of village and submitted the plaint in writing or reported the cause of dispute (Takrir) to the local authority. This was known as Karina. For instance, the complaint regarding the Deshpande watan of Taluka Khedebare during the rule of Shivaji is recorded in part three of Purandar daftar. It considerably helps in understanding the judicial procedure of the period of under-review. In the litigation of said watan of Khedebare,

Sakho Bhikaji, the plaintiff had appeared before King Shivaji and reported the dispute to him in writing.[1]

In this case, it is to be noted that the Agrawadi made the complaint to the king by appearing personally before him at Poona.[2] On hearing the plaint, King Shivaji seems to have referred the case to the pargana majlis. He issued one letter (rokha) in the name of Mukund Dhondadev Atre and the hawaldar and Bavaji Janardhan Majumdar and another letter was issued in the name of the Deshmukh for deciding the dispute. On receiving the plaint from the Agrawadi, the Deshmukh summoned Chimanaji Bapuji, the defendant and advised him to go to other place to decide the case.[3] Another complaint was lodged with the pargana officer of Supe, namely Ramji Babaji Deshpande by Malhar Babaji, Timaji Malhar and Trimbak Gomdeu, regarding the dispute of Deshmukhi watan arose between Sambahaji Kate and Samram Kate.[4] It is to be noted that both the litigants gave their consent for deciding the case with the help of pargana majlis presiding over it by the officer like Deshmukh. The Kazi and the Deshpande were to act as the witnesses. Both the litigants agreed to accept the verdict to be declared by the pargana majlis. In another dispute regarding Shete watan of peth, Murtazabad near Purandar arose between Datsheti and Shivasheti, the plaintiff, lodged a complaint with government officer and a Kasba (peth) majlis was summoned for trying the case. Both the parties (Agrawadi and Pashchimadi) submitted their consent in writing called as "rajinama" to the officer of the path (Shete) and agreed that the dispute between them should be tried by the Gota through majlis of Sawanzadia and be decided by presiding judges of pargana majlis like the Deshmukh and the Deshpande. The document called as "Rajinama" taken from the plaintiff was affixed by the persons like Umaji Naik Deshmukh of Saswad, Tukoji Zabira, mokadam of village Mujeri etc., acting as witnesses. Another written agreement given by the defendant was signed by Mauji

Deshmukh of Saswad and Tukoji Zabira, the mokadam of Mujeri as witnesses to his willingness.[5]

Jurisdiction of the Majlis

It seems that the jurisdiction of the majlis was determined by taking into account the place of complainant and the witnesses. The preference was given to the willingness of the plaintiff for appearing to the majlis to which he desires to decide his case. The litigant making complaint could appear to the officer of the place to which he belonged to or where the quarrel originated. For example, Timaji Khanderao who resided at Poona, lodged a complaint against Pandarkar brothers and made a request to him to decide the case of the Kulkarni watan of mauje Kolhale with the help of pargana Gota.[6]

Kathala meant Dispute regarding the Claim

When a person claimed over the watan enjoyed by another man then that watan became a disputable thing. The plaintiff who made a demand to a claim over the watan was the claimant and the man who refusd his claim was called paschimwadi or defendant. For instance, the plaintiffs such as Purushottambhat Haribhat, Vishwanathbat Atole made their demand to their claim over the watan of Upadhy, but their claim was denied by Govindbhat Ramana, the defendant. Thus, the Kathala or dispute regarding the watan of Upadhye of Taluka Devalekasba was originated.[6a]

Paksha or Parties

In a dispute in which the inhabitants of two villages had their interest or their rights were involved in common place, on such occasion, all those villagers were called as parties. For instance, in month of October 1658, a dispute over the boundary of two villages namely Kalbauli and Ravade arose in which the inhabitants of two villages were interested. Arjoi Dhamala and all the Deshaks of Paun Mawal, Hawaji Kalboli etc., involved in the dispute made the complaint to the Government officer at Purandar. All those inhabitants would be called as parties.[6b]

Mahzar

The verdict to be declared by the majlis was called as mahzar on which the names and designations of the members of the majlis were mentioned. For the final decision, the majlis took much time and then prepared the mahzar. Usually, the majlis gave judgement after two or four meetings.

Spot of Meeting of the Majlis

The chief officer of the territorial unit summoned the meeting of the majlis (court) in the temple of goddess "Shree of the village[7] or at the place of village called Pandhari[8] or on the plinth constructed round the trees of fig.[9] The Gota majlis used to decide the civil cases by examining the written evidences or by conducting oral enquiry about the case. The Gota through majlis tried to administer justice by going into the merits of the cases or examining the documents possessed by the litigants. It tried the cases with the help of witnesses and then could reach the final judgement. The majlis examined the documents carefully, determined their truthness and recognized their falseness correctly. With an aim of ascertaining of the truth, the expert men in law called as prashnik made an enquiry into the cases.

Presence of the Litigants before the Majlis was necessary

The defendant was asked to remain present before the majlis when it was required so. But if he refused or failed to appear before the members of the Gota then the latter could give decision against him and same judgement would lead to the dismissal of defendant's claim over the watan also. For instance, in October 1775, A.D., the Gotasabha of mauja Pasini consisting of Patil, Deshmukh, Kulkarni and mahar balutas asked Chandrabhat to be present before it for making an enquiry about the dispute of Kulkarni watan arose between him and Sindbhat. But Chandrabhat who was deprived of his right of Kulkarni watan remained absent at the time of the investigation of the case by the members of the majlis. The majlis administered justice in favour of Sindbhat, the winner of the case. Similarly, when Kauji Khandoji Garud, the plaintiff made a complaint against Haraji Mali and Mauji Mali regarding the mokadami watan to the Gotasabha of mauje Sikarpur in Junnar prant, the Hazir majlis asked Mauji Mali to be present before it for the investigation. But the defendant who could not appear before the majlis in time had to lose his claim over the mokadami watan as was declared by the Gota and the Gotapati, the head of the village Majlis.[11]

Oath

With a view that the person giving his witness before the majlis, should not give false statements, an oath was administered to him. The officers of the king had power to summon the witnesses. In presence of the members of the Gotamajlis and government officials, the witnesses had to swear by a cow or by their forefathers[12] etc. On some occasions, they had to administer an oath before the idol of the goddess etc. In deciding the dispute between Das Patil Malwadkar and Suryaji Adjoji Malwadkar, persons such as Rayaji Babaji, Baji Yekoji, Sindoji Malseti-Mahajan, Babaji Parasaram, Khanaji Tamboli, Kulkarni and Joshi, More Vishnu Belsare, Babaji Parasaram etc., were summoned at Purandar to give their witnesses in presence of Baji Gholap, the hawaldar and Sarnobat, Naikwadi of fort Purandar. Before giving evidence the witnesses were administered oath of their ancestors and leaves, flowers, turmeric dust, used for the worship of the goddess.[13]

Evidence and Ordeal

Yajnavalkya[14] has prescribed three types of evidences viz ; i) Writing, ii) Possession, iii) Witness. The fourth form is an ordeal which is prescribed in absence of any one of above mentioned evidences. Yajnavalkya further states that if there are witnesses or evidences in writing ordeal should not be performed.

It is worthy to be noted that ordeal is to be resorted to in case of important disputes[15] only. The evidence used for declaring the judicial verdict in Kingdom of Shivaji was of two kinds, i) human evidence, ii) ordeal. In the former included the documents Gohi, witness and possession etc. The judicial authorities in Maratha Kingdom also followed the ancient practice of trial by ordeals. When the documentary evidences or witnesses were not available this form of trial was adopted. There were various kinds of ordeals such as Agnidivya, Airanidivya etc. Fire as the means of evidence was used in Agnidivya. In form of Ravadivya, heated metal or iron balls were brought in use. For understanding of the procedure of the ordeals, some instances are described as under.

Ordeal of Water

In this form of ordeal the person was to plung into the deep water of a big pit of a river and was to catch thing thrown into the water. In contemporary records, some details about an ordeal are found as given below. Naroba Belsare who made a complaint to the government officer regarding the Kulkarni watan of the village Sakurde, appeared before Salabatkhan for administering justice with the help of an ordeal of water. Salabatkhan threw one coin (Sika) into the big pit of river filled with deep water and asked the accused (Naroba Belsara) to find out the Sika. The latter plunged into water and caught the same coin from the water of river pit. Thus he was cleared of guilty. On the contrary the mokadam of Sakurda was declared as guilty and Kulkarni watan was granted in the name of Belsara.[16]

Rava Ordeal

The details of this form of ordeal can better be explained by citing an example found in our sources. The plaintiff namely Visaji Naroba Masawada and Nagoji Kodbhat Patwardhan, the defendant, had performed an ordeal in the following manner. Both the persons arrived at Kedarsthan for performing an ordeal. On the festival day, Visaji Masawade made the preparation for ordeal by washing his hands with the help of lemon and soap. In same manner the defendant also washed his hands. Then their hands were bandaged. Later on, they took the bath at Kedarnath and worshipped the goddess of Nandakeshwar and Kedareshwar on an ordeal day. Then some mixed ghee and oil were heated and then poured into the metal pot. A piece of iron was thrown into boiled ghee and oil. After then, Visaji Narayan, the plaintiff took out the piece of iron kept in heated oil and ghee. The same action was performed by the defendant namely Nagoji Patvardhan. On third day i.e. on Tuesday, all the members of assembly were summoned to examine the hands of those persons. The bandages from their hands were taken off. After examining the palms of both men, the hands of plaintiff were found without injury or with no new signs. Hence Visaji Narayan was pronounced as true and Nagoji Patvardhan as guilty by the assembly.[17] Another example that can be cited is that of Ajoji Jasojirao who performed Rava ordeal. The truth regarding the mokadami watan of mauje Salasi was tested by undergoing Rava ordeal by Alojirao and Tanajirao Kandatkar. Both the persons were sent to the place where the ordeal was to take place. Each one of them was given a iron ball. On Saturday of December, 1657, the preparation for an ordeal was made by washing the hands of the persons who had to perform an ordeal in presence of government officers and the members of Hazar Majlis. Next day, i.e. on Sunday, the meeting of the majlis held in the temple of goddess Shree Hanmant and there mixed quantity of two and half seers of oil and ghee was boiled in the pot in which a piece of iron was thrown. The accused was askd to take out that piece of metal from the heated oil and ghee. On that day, the plaintiff took the bath in holy water of the river. The tad patra declaring the cause for undergoing an ordeal was attached to the forehead of Alojirao. Then the piece of iron was thrown into the heated quantity of oil and ghee. The plaintiff put on his hand into the pot to take out the piece of iron from the heated liquid mixed together with oil and ghee. Then the hands of that person were bandaged and were covered with the cloth in presence of the hawaldar. Later on, on third day i.e., on Tuesday, in presence of Hazir Majlis, the bandage was broken and his palms were released. After examining his hands, it was found that Alojirao was declared as successful candidate. Because after having taken off the piece of iron from heated liquid, his palms were not burnt and thus Alojirao established his innocence.

Ordeal of Grain

In Rava ordeal, the black gram and white gram were also brought in use. For instance, Ramseti Setya and Seti Langseti Binge when performed Rava ordeal for ascertaining of the truth about Shete watan of Kasba Atapadi, they adopted following method. The black piece of gram and white piece of gram were selected for Rava ordeal. Both pieces were covered separately with the dust made from jwar. Those two pieces were thrown into rounded vessel filled with cold water. Then the plaintiff was asked to take out one of the pieces from the vessel. If the person takes out white gram from the vessel, he is true, if he gets the black gram then he is of guilty. Then Ramseti took out a white gram from the cold water and proved as true. Mangseti was declared as false.[19]

Divine Ordeal

On some of the occasions, the truth was tested by taking an oath of Belbhandar before the goddess. In this form of ordeal, the complainant was to swear on leaves of Bela tree and bhandar (turmeric powder). The procedure of this ordeal can be explained by citing the following instance. The Hasham Mulvawe people of mauje Kari in tarf Bortape Rohida performed an ordeal of Belbhandar by taking an oath of milk and boiled rice in the temple of Shri Raireshwar in order to ascertain the truth regarding the right over village watan.

Judicial Cases decided with the help of Ordeals

Name of Place	*Person who Performed Ordeal*	*Kind of Litigation*	*Judicial Body*	*Kind of Ordeal*	*Witness to Ordeal*
1	*2*	*3*	*4*	*5*	*6*
Kedarsthan in temple of goddess Kedar	Visaji[21] Narayan Masawade	Kulkarni Watan	Pargana Majlis at Saswad	Rava ordeal	Deshmukh
Kedarsthan in temple of goddess Kedar	Nagoji[22] Kotbhat Patvardhan	Kulkarni watan	Huzur Majlis	Ordeal of taking out metal from boiling oil	Hawaldar
Poona	Malaji[23] Bhalerao Sedakar	Mokadami Watan of mauje Nimbodi	Hazir Majlis at mauje Nimbodi	Rava ordeal	Hawaldar
Shree Dev Mahasthal Mauje Mohori Nasarapur	Janaji[24] Khaira	Mokadami watan of mauje Kodit	Hazir Majlisi at Kasaba Gota Khedebare	Rava ordeal	Deshmukh
Daulat Mangali	Narayan[25] Belsara	Kulkarni and Jyotisi watan	Hazir majlisi at Daulat Mangal	Ordeal of taking out metal from boiling ghee and oil	Deshmukh
In temple of Shree at Markasba	Mahad-nak[26] Bhiknak Mahar	Mahar vritti of Kasba Mar	Hazir Majlis	Rava ordeal	Deshmukh
On Pandhari of village Umbraj	Timaji[27] Pant	Patilki watan	Village Majlis	Three kinds of ordeals using lamps Bel & water	Patil and Thelari

Name of Place	Person who Performed Ordeal	Kind of Litigation	Judicial Body	Kind of Ordeal	Witness to Ordeal
1	2	3	4	5	6
In village temple of goddess Hanuman	Alojirao[28] Jasojirao Khandat-kar	Mokadami watan of Salasi	Hazir Majlis	Rava ordeal	Hawaldar
Poona	Tan[29] Patil	Patilki watan	Hazir Majlis at Poona	Rava ordeal	Deshmukh mokadams and village residents
Man Dahigaon	Rem[30] Sheti	Shete watan of Atapadi	Pargana Majlis	Grain ordeal	Hawaldar
Peth Shahapur of Kasba Poona (in temple of Nagesh)	Lakhad[31] Rana Somad Rana Gurav	Mokadami watan of mauje Bhiwari	Hazir Majlis	Rava ordeal	Deshmukh shete Mahajan Mokadams and Balutas of village

Offence and Penalty

King Shivaji followed rules laid down in Hindu Dharma Sastras for inflicting the punishments on the offenders. Numerous and various kinds of crimes committed by the offenders in Maratha Kingdom were as given below :

(i) Offence against king, (ii) Offence of defalcation, (iii) Adultery, (iv) Forgery, (v) Theft and Robbery, (vi) Offence relating to false witness, (vii) Offence of defamation, (viii) Corruption.

Offence against King

The offences such as causing injury to the king or making plots against the king or providing aid to the forces of the king etc., were considered as most serious offences[32] and different penalties were prescribed for them by the Dharma Sastras. For instance, Yashvantrao

Siwatarkar who disobeyed the king and helped Shivaji's enemy was blinded by the latter and was kept in confinement on fort.[33] The hawladar of Kudal pargana was strictly warned by the king to imprison the persons like Daulat Khohi who aided king's enemy and also acted as traitor against the ruler. The punishment of such men was left to the king who issued an order to the hawaldar to imprison such treacherous men.[34] Some of the Maratha nobles who became traitors were sent into the prison by the king.

Offence of Defalcation

The act of misappropriating of public money by the Government officers was subject to the punishment. Defalcation of revenue amount by the State officials was considered a serious offence. For instance, once Jivaji Vinayak, an officer of Prabhavali could not remit the amount of revenue collection to state's treasury and thus committed a crime of defalcation of public money.[35] Likewise Appaji Tawaji, the Deshkulkarni of mamle Cheul collected revenue from peasants, but did not keep a detailed account of revenue receipts. The officer thus used to defraud the king by misappropriating the revenue income of the State. The king after realising the offence declared the officer as guilty of defalcation of public money. The king punished the offender by confiscating his watan.

Cause of Adultery. Yajnavalkya says, if a man enjoys another man's wife forcibly, his act must be regarded as a heinous crime and punishment prescribed for such person is the confiscation of all his properties and also the punishment from town or kingdom.[36]

Cases of Adultery. Bawaji Bhikaji Gujar, the mokadam of mauje Ranze debauched a woman. King Shivaji punished the offender by confiscating his watan of mokadami and issued an order to cut off his legs and hands also.[37] Not only the men committing adultery were punished but also the women committing the same crime were liable for punishment. For instance, the wife of Suryaji Dunduskar's servant, once committed adultery when she arrived on Raigad. The tarfadar who investigated the case, punished the woman by imposing upon her a fine of fifty-seven rupees.[38] Rango Trimal Wakada, a village Kulkarni of Mauje Mosekhore forcibly committed intercourse with a Brahmin widow. On hearing of the news of the heinous act done by the Kulkarni, King Shivaji immediately gave an order to imprison the offender who had already fled to the territory of the king's foe[39] for shelter. Once, an army officer namely Sakhuji Gaikwad was accused for wicked deed of dishonouring the Desai woman.[40] He committed rape on Desai woman. After hearing the report about the evil deed of Sakhuji Gaikwad, King Shivaji issued an order to keep him in prison till the death. Again the criminal was severely punished by putting out his eyes.[41]

Forgery. The act of preparing forged documents relating to the watan or sale and purchase of land was considered as an offence. Subhanji Santaji of mauje Samanpur prepared a forged document showing the distribution of Patilwatan between him and Khandoji Deshmukh. The former blamed the latter for defrauding of fifty thousand rupees from the public money. But after examining the case, it was found that the documents relating to watan possessed by Shubhanji were forged. Therefore, he was imprisoned by King's officer for the crime.[42] Likewise, on making the complaint to the government by Wagoji Dhonda Patil, it was found that Hiroji had made forged writing about mokadami watan of Chikhalgaon and falsely claimed over that watan.[43] Another person namely Rangoji Patwari Chatorikar of pargana Gulshanabad had prepared a forged document claiming his right over half of Deshpande watan belonging to Krishnaji Agaria. After investigating into the case, it came to know that Ranaji forcibly took a written document from the latter showing his claim over half of the said watan. But in fact, he did not pay the price of the half of the watan to Krishnaji.[44] When Khandoji Malaji Deshmukh was busy in his work on Raigad, the Deshmukhi watan was equally distributed between Bhivaji Mahska and Nagoji Deshmukh. In absence of Khandoji, Bhivaji had made a forged document to be written by force from the wife of the former and showed his claim over twelve villages and land which actually did not belong to him.[45] Similarly, Timaji Khanderao of Jejuri made a complaint to the king that Rakhamaji Unda and Antaji Unda Kulkarni of mauje Kolhale forcibly made a written document from him showing that the Jyotisi or Kulkarni watan was sold out to them during the days of famine by the complainant for the price of twenty hons.[46]

Offence of Murder

In contemporary records, we find some cases of death caused by various means. Yakub had killed the father of Narsoji Jagadale of tarf Masur. Jagdale also took revenge by killing two Muslims namely Majawar.[47] Vitthal Kai Deu was killed by the father of Ramaji Kulkarni who was killed by unknown person.[48] Apaji Deshmukh was murdered by Ramaji by offering him poison.[49] Sarjerao, the son of Haibatrao was murdered by Dhamale Deshmukh of prant Malwal.[50] Khandoji Desai of Rohida killed the mother of Kedarji Desai.[51] Ramaji was murdered by Dadajipant[52] in 1647. Harba and Ramji were murdered by a Deshmukh of Rajpur by beating and poisoning them respectively.[53] Tabajipant in Akole pargana was killed by Hauji Deshmukh[54] by giving him poison, in 1664 A.D. Bhanaji Kulkarni of mauje Nimbut was killed by Atoji Nigada.[55] Takawane caused the deaths of six persons.[56] Surarkhan killed Timaji at Daulatabad.[57]

In the following table the cases of murder caused by different means and found in our records of the period under review have been shown.

Murder of	*Caused by*	*No. of Persons*
Murder of Hindu person	beating	1
Murder of the Muslims	beating	2
Vitthal Kai Deu	killing	1
Apaji Deshmukh	poisoning	1
Sarjerao	beating	1
Rayarao	armed man	1
Mother of Medarji Desai	beating	1
Ramaji	beating	1
Tubaji Pant Deshmukh	poisoning	1
Ramaji Deshmukh	poisoning	1
Harba	beating	1
Bhanaji Kulkarni	killing	1
Takawane	beating	6
Timaji	beating	1

False Witness

Giving false evidence was regarded as offence. Yajnavalkya has prescribed penances to the persons who gave false witnesses.[58] Manu says that giving a false witness is equal to the crime of killing of a fraud.[59] Yajnavalkya has also prescribed in a fine of some amount of rupees from those persons who gave false witnesses in the litigation.[60] But sometimes, the witnesses due to fear, gave false statements too. Thus, for instance in 1654 A.D., Kedaraji Ravalaji Zabira, who was afraid of beating by Tukoji Dhangar resorted to falsehood and gave the evidence regarding the patilki watan of mauje Pede in favour of the latter.[61]

Robbery and Plunder

In Maratha Kingdom the plunder and robbery disturbing the peaceful life of society and causing sufferings to a large number of people were punished by

King Shivaji. The noble man of Adilshah namely Haibatkhan once plundered everything from Kanadkhore of Satara made an assault on mauje Sayagaon in tarf Madhe and plundered the animals of village. The state issued them warning and abstained them from doing so.[63] Similarly the robbers committing robbery were severely punished by the state.

Jangappa Bhil, one of the robbers who disturbed peaceful life always threatened the people and made them afraid of him. The Government caught him by sending the regiment of troops and seized him and kept in confinement.[64] Chitnis Bakhar mentions that Shivaji gave severe punishment to robbers and thieves and tried to make his kingdom free from robbery and theft.[64]

Offence of Defamation and Insult

Causing harm to one's reputation was regarded as crime in kingdom of Shivaji. In 1662 A.D. a boy belonging to Rajput caste defamed Pantaji Pandit the learned and respectable envoy at the court of Shivaji. The king issued a letter of warning to Rajaji, the Rajput Deshmukh making him aware of the consequences of dishonouring of king's ambassador Pantaji. For the defamation of a learned scholar the king warned his officer to inflict the punishment of putting iron rings on the feet of the offender and to send him into the prison.[65]

Offence of Corruption

Corruption among government officials was regarded as serious crime. Manu says that the officers of king who were deputed to investigate the cases, if received bribes from one of the parties involved in disputes should be punished by king by confiscating all their property.[66] We have a typical instance in which the hawaldar of mahal indulged in bribery and delivered wrong judgement that favoured the bribe giver. The complainant who appealed to King Shivaji for justice requested him to decide the matter in person. King Shivaji who made an investigation thoroughly into the case and found out the truth that

Pandarkar brothers had bribed the officer. The king prescribed severe punishments such as confiscation of watan and imprisonment for the officer as well as for the bribe giver.[67] Another instance of an offence of bribery committed by the government officer is that of Naroba an officer of Poona pargana, who accepted the bribe for the decision regarding the dispute of Patil watan between Ravaji Patil and Sonaji Tupe. The officer gave judgement in favour of the former who gave him one hundred and twenty-five hons,[68] as bribe. Some of the officers of the forts also demanded bribe from the prisoners for their release. An officer of Kharpatan fort who was ordered by Shivaji to release the captives from the prison, did not set them free and desired a bribe from the captives for their release from imprisonment.[69] Dishonesty and all the corrupt practices were regarded as crimes and were subject to the various punishments.

Authority to Forgive

King Shivaji possessed the power to forgive. In fact, it was one of his prerogatives. The king issued a letter to Haibatrau Silambkar who acted treacherously against him and was exiled. Sambhaji, the brother of an offender made a request to the king to forgive his brother who was subjugated before him. Therefore, King Shivaji accepted the request and forgave the offender.[70]

Forms of Punishment

Regarding punishment Manu says, "The king cannot justly administer punishment alone by himself without the assistance of councillors, army commanders and administrators of justice.[71]

Fines

The main feature of this penalty was that no amount was fixed for that. But it is obvious that the heavy amount was imposed upon accused for the serious offence and a lenient fine was levied for ordinary one. If the litigant disobeyed the decision given by the Gotasabha, he was to be punished with heavy fine of five hundred hons.[72] Even if some one tried to bring obstacle in implementing the judgement of the Gota, he was punished with five hons.[73] Heavy fines were imposed upon the offenders committing intercourse forcibly with others' women. A wife of a servant having committed an immoral intercourse with other person was fined with fifty-seven rupees by the officer of the tarf. A watandar committing the murder was punished by the king with two hundred hons and his half of patil watan was confiscated from him.[75] Bavaji Bhikaji who committed heinous act of dishonouring other's woman was fined with three hundred hons and had lost his physical organs such as legs, hands etc.[76] The person who failed to prove his claim over the watan and falsely claimed over the same Watan was fined with some amount of hons.[77] But the offender committing the murder of his opponent by cutting off his head was punished with heavy fine of five hundred hons.[78]

Imprisonment

It is to be noted that the period of the imprisonment was never determined. A rebellious person, acting against Shivaji was imprisoned on the fort for many years.[79] Sonprabhu and Mahadu Prabhu were imprisoned in the fort for making quarrel with each other.[80] A mokadam namely Valhekar Barwoji, who killed Bal Joshi, a village Kulkarni of mauje Walhe, in Poona prant was seized by the Hawaldar of Shirwal and sent him into the prison. Again, he was fined with a heavy amount of hons.[81] A person insulting a respectable man in court was imprisoned by putting iron rings on his feet.[82] Naikaji Ambaji who plundered the treasury that was carried away to Bijapur was kept in confinement and later on his head was cut off by the officer of the Adilshah.[83]

Mutilation

The punishment of mutilation was inflicted in cases of wicked deed of dishonouring the woman,[84] misbehaviour with other's ladies.[85] The treacherous persons or men acting against the rule of their master, could become victims of king's wrath. And their hands, feet[86] were cut off or eyes were put out.[87] The man failing in performing the Rava ordeal successfully was punished with lenient fine.

Capital Punishment

Death penalty might be prescribed for the severe crimes such as plundering of royal treasury, forming conspiracy against king, killing of men and women, adultery etc. We found no evidence to the cases of capital punishment inflicted upon the criminals in his kingdom by the king. We did not come across any evidence in our records of crushing of the offenders to death beneath the feet of elephants or beheading them etc. Death punishment would not be inflicted without the approval of the king.[88]

Court Fee

The litigants involved in dispute were to pay some amount as court fee. Serani was a sort of court fee to be paid by the person who won the case and Haraki was paid by the litigant who was the loser. In the dispute over the Mahar Vritti Mahadnak who agreed to perform the Rava ordeal had to pay fifty takas as Serani,[89] if he would win the suit. He also gave his consent to pay one hundred and fifty takas as gunehgari in case if he would lose the case. In such cases, the amount of court fee collected from loser party was three times more than the amount levied from the winner. But in case of a dispute regarding the watan of Dharmadhikari Joshi who was the loser, had to pay fifty hons as gunehgari whereas Nabhibhat paid only twenty-five hons as Servani to the government. In this case, the amount to be levied from the loser was double than that of the fee collected from the winner party.[90] But on rare occasions, the fee collected from the offender was ten times more than that of the amount levied from the accused.[91]

Legal Rights Enjoyed by Women in Swaraj

It appears that the ideas of Hindu Dharma Shastras had been rooted deeply in society of Swaraj under Shivaji. The principles in Shastras had conferred upon the women some legal rights too. Some women in medieval Maharashtra had been enjoying the rights and privileges of holding watan. For instance, after the death of Baji, the Shete of the peth Azamgad near Murtazabad his wife namely Gaurai who was really a competent lady, conducted the administration of the watan, held the office of Shete of the peth and thus was enjoying all the rights over such watan.[92] Similarly, the royal woman like Ausaheb, Jijabai, mother of King Shivaji was competent to preside over the meeting of Hazir Majlasi Gota at Dhanib of taluka Kanadkhore. The meeting of Gota was called in month of January 1667, to administer justice to Babaji Deshmukh and Maloji Patangrao Deshmukh of Kanadkhore.[93] It should be remembered that woman could also be a witness in disputed cases of watan. For example, Tukai Deshmukhin of pargana Shirwal attended the Hazir Majlasi of pargana level and acted as one of the members of judicial body.[94] After the death of father, a daughter would also be the claimant of the watan of her father. When the person died without male issue, his daughter or son-in-law would enjoy the same watan.

Thus, from above given evidence it cannot be denied that some qualified and competent women in medieval Maharashtra had been occupying not only considerable high status, but they were also enjoying the legal rights on equal footing with the gentlemen in society of those times.

REFERENCES AND FOOTNOTES

1. Deshpande Taluka Khedebare Yancha Shivkalin Karina, Purandare Daftar, III, P. 130
2. Ibid, P. 132
3. Ibid, P. 134
4. MIS, XX, Letter No. 18
5. SCS, II, Letter No. 103
6. Ibid, 7, PP. 68-69

6a SPSS, Letter No. 1829

6b Chaturtha Sammelan, Vritta, P. 79

7. MIS XX, PP. 83 and 89
8. Gune V. T. Op cit, P. 74
9. Ibid P. 202
10. SCS, II, Letter No. 110
11. Aitihasik Sankirna Sahitya, Part VIII, Letter No. 30
12. SCS II, Letter No. 96, P. 121
13. Ibid, 7, Letter No. 57, P. 97
14. Vishwanath Narayan Mandlik Vyavahara Mayukh and Yajnavalkya Smriti, Part II, P. 15
15. Ibid, Part II, P. 210
16. SCS 7, P. 29
17. SCS, I, P. 10
18. Ibid, III, PP. 230-231
19. Gune V. T. Op cit, PP. 266-67
20. SCS, II, PP. 326-327
21. SCS, I, Letter No. 9
22. Ibid, I, Letter No. 11
23. Ibid, I, Letter No. 22
24. Ibid, I, Letter No. 26
25. Ibid, 7, Letter No. 21
26. Ibid, 7, Letter No. 43
27. MIS XX, Letter No. 181
28. SCS, III, PP 230 and 231
29. MIS, XVIII, Letter No. 3
30. Gune V. T. Op cit, P. 154
31. SCS, V, Letter No. 873
32. Ibid, II, Letter No. 253
33. Ibid, II, Letter No. 253
34. Ibid, II, PP 323-324
35. MIS, VIII, Letter No. 31
36. Vishwanath Narayan Mandlik, Vyavahara Mayukha. In original with English translation, Yajnavalkya Smriti, Part I and II, P. 149
37. SPSS, I, Letter No. 510
38. MIS, VIII, Letter No. 32
39. MIS, XV, Letter No. 270
40. Tarikhe Shivaji quoted in Pagadi's Op cit, P. 292

41. 91 Qalami Bakhar, P. 144
42. SCS, III, P. 82
43. SPSS, III, Letter No. 2490
44. Ibid, III, Letter No. 2637
45. SCS, III, Letter No. 475, P. 81
46. Ibid, II, Letter No. 140
47. SPSS, I, Letter No. 50
48. SCS, I, PP. 31-32
49. Ibid, I, Letter No. 25
50. SPSS III, Letter No. 2429
51. Ibid III, Letter No. 2571
52. Ibid, III, Letter No. 2523
53. SCS, III, Letter No. 466
54. Ibid, III, Letter No. 464
55. Ibid, I, Letter No. 48
56. Ibid, II, Letter No. 98
57. SPSS, III, Letter No. 2637
58. Mandlik V. N., Vyavahara Mayukh and Yajnayalkya Smriti, Part II, P. 30
59. Manu Smriti, The Laws of Manu with the Bhasya of Medhatithi, Vol, III, Part II, P. 383
60. Mandlik V. N., The Vyavahara Mayukha. In original with the English translation. The Yajnavalkya Smriti, Part I and II, P. 25
61. SCS, III, Letter No 638, PP. 224-225
62. SPSS, III, Letter No. 2392
63. Ibid, III, Letter No. 2568
64. Ibid, III, Letter No. 2484

64a Chitnis Bakhar, P. 115

65 SPSS III, Letter No. 2663

66. Ganganath Jha, Manusmriti, The Laws of Manu with the Bhasya of Medhatithi, Vol. II, Part-II, P. 186
67. SCS, 7, Letter No. 44
68. SPSS, III, Letter No. 778
69. English Records on Shivaji I, Letter Nos. 7 & 8
70. SCS, II, Letter No. 253
71. Ganganath Jha, Manu Smriti, The Laws of Manu with the Bhasya of Medhatithi, Vol. III, Part II, P. 292
72. SCS, I, P. 48
73. MIS XX, P. 94

74. Tarikhe Shivaji, quoted in Pagadi's Op cit, P. 292
75. MIS, VIII, Letter No. 32
76. SCS, II, P. 126
77. CSP, Letter No. 4
78. SCS, I, P. 41
79. Ibid, II, Letter No. 253
80. Ibid, P. 295
81. SPSS, I, Letter No. 732
82. Ibid, III, 2663
83. MIS, XX, P. 264
84. 91 Qalami Bakhar P. 144
85. SCS, II, P. 240
86. CSP, Letter No. 4
87. 91 Qalami Bakhar P. 144
88. MIS, XX, P. 265
89. SCS 7, P. 63
90. MIS, XX, P. 281
91. Ibid XX, P 335
92. SCS, II, Letter No. 103, P. 133
93. MIS, XVI, Letter No. 22
94. SCS, I, Letter No. 19, P. 31

7

Conclusion

It appears from the discussion in preceding Chapters that the responsibility of impartial justice ultimately fell upon King Shivaji who was the supreme authority in administering justice to the litigants. It is obviously true that the judicial courts in Swaraj under Shivaji were organised with a view of promoting the welfare of his subjects and their happiness. Though there might be some faults in judicial system under Shivaji, yet as a king, he certainly acted as a human towards the people. It seems that wherever and whenever socio-religious and economic conditions permitted, the judicial authorities at the centre and local level, made definite attempts to give justice to the persons on the principles mentioned by the Dharma Shastras which not only afforded the sanctity to the judicial judgements, but also laid stress on the impartiality of the judges of courts. The king followed the Hindu laws prescribed by the Shastras in the administration of justice in his state. In civil cases, principles laid down in the books like Vidnyaneshwar were applied when the dispute between the Hindu and Muslim litigants was to be decided.[1]

Similarly, the practice of performing an ordeal was applied to the Muslim when a dispute between two litigants of Muslim community arose. For instance, for deciding the case of Alojirao Muslim who had a quarrel with Tanaji Chandroji Kandatkar over the mokadami watan, Rava ordeal was applied and he was advised to perform it for investigating the truth when testimonial evidences were not available.[2] In cases of disputes, relating to the watan, money and property distribution of father's wealth and property etc., Hindu laws laid down in Dharmashastras were applied and vedic scholars residing at holy places were consulted for giving the decisions. The administration of justice under King Shivaji indicates that the religious factor also exercised influences over the judiciary of his kingdom. Whenever the written or oral evidences were not available, the performance of an ordeal by litigant was followed with a view to administer justice to him.

In connection with the courts, it can be said that from village level to the pargana or Subha, the Gotasabhas were functioning like courts. It appears that there was a well organization of judicial bodies from central court, the highest authority to the lowest judicial body of the Gotasabha of the village. The rural as well as urban people were enjoying the freedom to decide their disputes with the help of the Gotasabha. They could appear before King Shivaji for justice only when they required or only when it made them necessary to have the decision from the king. It is a thing of worth noting here that in the larger interest of the people, King Shivaji permitted all types of social communities, cases and their representatives to be associated in the provincial administration of justice. Gota Majlis was a sort of democratic body consisting of the representatives or a council consisting of the representatives of village residents assembled for giving judgements on the disputes arose in the territory of jurisdiction. The Gotamajlis was not only a democratic body, it was also a decision making council of village. Because the significant business of the justice was transacted at its meeting. All the members who were present there enjoyed the right of expressing their opinions. The Gota Majlis which was the gathering of selected and prominent men of all sections in society, discussed all sorts of issues involved in disputes. The village residents, higher and lower watandars were its members and attended its meetings. The Government officer who seated in a chair granted permission to every member to express his opinion and received his report. Thus, the Gotamajlis was nothing more than the judicial court whose chief business was to declare judgement on the suits brought before it. King Shivaji was eager to see that the judges of the courts should be active in administering the justice and should not delay the judgements. The Subha majlis and Gota majlis examined the cases brought before them thoroughly. The policy of King Shivaji was not to interfere in the judicial decisions given by the Gota Majlis. On the contrary, he had recognised its authority and sanctity. Hence, he referred many cases for trial to the Gotasabha[3] and always preferred not to interfere in its judgement.

Hindu Dharmashastras made the king the highest authority to administer justice to the people in his kingdom. The essential duty of the king was to afford protection and to prove impartial justice to his subjects. The highest court of justice in the kingdom was the Chhatrapati and his council of Ministers. The King had devoted his valuable time to hear the complaints when the agrawadi appeared before him to tell the grievances. He not only heard the cases but also listened the appeals. He had judicial courts, thus from Subha downwards in each pargana or tarf, Kasba, headquarters throughout his kingdom.

Shivaji's love of justice can be revealed from the evidences that he was strict in punishing his officers against whom complaints of injustice were reported to the king. Shivaji deprived the officer of his watan at once when his guilt was proved.[4] In the interest of social justice and prosperity of the subjects, the criminals were dealt with heavily by the king. He also issued strict instructions to the officials to arrange for prompt action against the offenders and administer justice impartially and promptly. The object of inflicting the severe penalties upon the offenders for different crimes was to create the fear in their minds and to prevent them from committing further more crimes.

The main characteristic of the judiciary under his rule was that he did not think justice as a source of monetary gain to the king and never allowed the injust to prosper in the Maratha Kingdom. The people had direct access to King Shivaji who heard the complaints of his subjects. He was succeeded to do so and could stand high in the eyes of his people. King Shivaji's sense of justice was really high and can be proved by the case of one of his wife's relatives. The king had learnt that the offender had committed an act of corruption. Shivaji investigated the case personally. When the accused found guilty in an investigation, the king ordered to keep him into the prison till his death. Shivaji was most particular in context of justice and took an active interest in administering justice personally. He was quite anxious, keen and firm in dealing justice to his officials.

Therefore, the reign of Shivaji can be admired as a period of impartiality and stern policy towards justice. King Shivaji was more zealous to meet out justice to his men. He made no distinction of rank, or position of the accused and inflicted punishments on offenders freely. In this regard, the case cited was that of Sakhuji Gaikwad who committed an act of rape on helpless woman of defeated enemy. The complaint was brought before the king, who ordered to put out the eyes of the criminal officer and keep him in prison till his death. The incident took place when the Maratha army was returning from the military campaign. Shivaji had no hesitation in pronouncing the judgement against his army officer or in favour of the enemy's woman. It is really a matter of pride that the judgement King Shivaji pronounced was executed on the spot where the incident happened. In fact, the decision shows that the king seems to have made it a rule that the penalty of the offender should be carried out immediately after proving of the guiltiness of the person.

If or whenever it came to the knowledge of King Shivaji that any of his officers had been guilty of oppression, he first of all gave him warning and then inflicted the severe punishment on him. He wanted that his subjects should be happy and contented. He desired them to be free completely from the oppressiveness of state officers. To make it more clear how exceedingly he was careful in governing his kingdom and administering the justice to his people, one can well remember the instructions issued by the Chhatrapati to his officials. The instructions issued by the king in 1673 A.D., to his officers of mamle Dabhol, can better help us to understand the ideal of his justice and his objective to protect the poor peasants from officer's oppression and injustice. Those letters also reveal king's anxiety for the cultivators. The King instructed his soldiers and army officers not to take away the foodgrains, vegetables, and other necessaries of daily life from peasants forcibly. He made them aware by bringing into their notice that if they misbehaved with the subjects, the latter might think that the Maratha troops were not better than the Mughals.[5] To Shivaji, justice meant dharma, righteous act, or justice in accordance with Dharma Shastras. Hence he was more conscious in regard to the justice and performed the judicial duty to the best of his ability.

His officials were empowered to administer justice, but sometimes, the decisions of his subordinate officers were liable to be revised or modified by Shivaji himself.[6] Important drawback of the judiciary of the Maratha state under Shivaji may be noticed in corruption of the judicial officers. For instance, we can consider the case of Naroba, the judicial officer of Poona pargana who was bribed with an amount of one hundred and twenty-five hons for deciding the suit in favour of Rayaji Patil.[7] It appears that bribery and corruption were rampant among some officials who administered justice to the people. Other weakness of Shivaji's judiciary was the penalty of confinement. The forts were used as prisons. The officers used those forts for the imprisonment of their opponents against whom they had personal grievances. Moreover, the arrangement in prisons provided to criminals was worse. Again the period of confinement for particular crime was not fixed by certain rules or the regulations. The hawaldar had right to send the offender into prison for committing an offence for which imprisonment was prescribed by the king. The punishment of confinement was inflicted upon the officials or individuals who found guilty of accepting bribe, making fraud in government treasury and for acting as a false witness. Some of the faults or deficiencies which were lying in judiciary of the period under review, were the result of socio-economic structure of the Maratha society existed in those days, but mainly they were the outcome of the lucre and qualities of the persons performing the judicial duties. A few officials acting as judicial head of the territorial unit forgot their status, responsibility. A few of them lacked the efficiency for administering justice with honesty.[8] It is true that the king did not try to reform the judicial system into which some notable defects had crept. As a matter of fact, Shivaji must not be condemned merely because he did not innovate the new principles of justice or failed to prepare new laws of his own. But he can be amply justified on the ground that in achieving his political aim, the king had no spare time to bring reforms in the judicial branch of his state administration.

REFERENCES AND FOOTNOTES

1. Gune V.T., JSM, P 152
2. SCS III, Letter No. 639
3. SCS II, Letter No. 98, also see Gune V.T. Op. cit., PP. 197-198
4. SCS 7, Letter No 44

5. MIS, VIII, Letter No. 28
6. MIS XVII, Letter No. 10
7. SPSS III, Letter No. 2778
8. SCS, 7, Letter No. 44

Bibliography

Marathi Chronicles

Sabhasad Bakhar : Krishnaji Anant Sabhasad.

Virchit : Shiv Chhatrapatiche Charitra edited by R.V. Herwadkar, Pune, 1986.

Sabhasad Bakhar, edited by V.S. Wakaskar, Pune, 1962.

Shri Shivchhatrapatiche Saptprakarnatmak Charitra by Malhar Ramrao Chitnis.

Edited by Prof. Bhimrao Kulkarni, Pune, 1967.

Shri Shiv-digvijay edited by Dhere R.C., Pune, 1975.

91 Qalami Bakhar, edited by V.S. Wakaskar, Pune, 1962.

Ancient Hindu Law Books

Manu Smriti : The laws of Manu with the Bhasya of Medhatithi, translated by Ganganath Jha, Vol, III, Part II, Calcutta University, 1924.

Manu Dharmasastra: Translated by George Buhler, Oxford, 1886.

Narad Smriti : The Minor Law Books translated by Julins Jolly, Oxford, 1889.

Gautama Dharmasutras, translated by George Buhler, Oxford, 1879.

Baudhayana Dharmasutras, translated by George Buhler, Oxford, 1882.

Yajnavalkya Smriti with Apararka's Commentary, Anandasram Series, 1903.

Yajnavalkya Smriti : Part I & II. By Vishwanath Narayan Mandlik, Education Society's Press. Bombay, 1880.

History of Dharma Sastra : P.V. Kane, 4 Vols. Poona, 1935-53.

Dharmasastras : Translation of Smritis. Dutta M.N.

The Sacred Books of the Hindus : The Sukraniti, Vol. VIII, Edited by Basu.

Yajnavalkya Smriti with Mitakshara : Narayan Ram Acharya, Bombay

Vyavahara Mayukh and Yajnavalkya Smriti : Parts I, II. Mandlik, V.N.

Sanskrit Sources

Vyavaharanirnaya by Gagabhatta : Manuscript copy is available in Bhandarkar Oriental Research Institute, Poona.

The work throws considerable light on ordeals and oaths and describes the procedure of administering justice in detail.

Keshav Pandit's Dandaniti : The original work has been written by the author in Sanskrit. The work gives the information on criminal jurisprudence of the 17th century Maharashtra. It has been edited by Dr. V.S. Bendrey and published by Bharat Itihas Sanshodhak Mandal, Poona, in 1943.

Ajna Patra : edited by S. N. Banhatti, Pune, 1961.

Official Letters and Documents

Shiva Charitra Sahitya, Vols. 1 to 14, Bharat Itihas Sanshodhak Mandal, Poona.

Purandare Daftar, edited by K.V. Purandare, Part III, Pune, 1934.

Shivakalin Patrasar Sangrah, Vols. 1 to 3, Bharat Itihas Sanshodhan Mandal, Poona.

The Records of the Shivaji's period, edited by V.G. Khobrekar, Bombay, 1974.

Marathyanchya Itihasachi Sadhane, edited by V.K. Rajwade, Parts 8, 15, 16, 17 and 20.

Chhatrapati Shivaji Maharajanchi Patre, edited by P.N. Deshpande, Dhule, 1983.

Maharashtracha Patrarup Itihas, edited by D. V. Apte, and R. V. Oturkar, Poona, 1941.

Aitihasik Sankirn Sahitya, Parts 1 and 3 and 8.

Modern Works

Ahmad M. Bashir, Administration of Justice in Medieval India, Aligarh, 1941.

Altekar A. S., State and Government in Ancient India, Varanasi, 1972.

Chapekar N.G., Marathirajyatil Nyayapadhati, Desai Commemoration Volume.

Day U.N., The Government of the Sultanate, New Delhi, 1972.

Day U.N., The Mughal Government, New Delhi, 1970.

Dikshitar V. R., Hindu Administrative Institutions.

Damayanti Doongaji, Law of Crime and Punishment in Ancient Hindu Society.

Gune V. T., Judicial system of the Marathas, Poona, 1953.

Ibn Hasan, The Central Structure of the Mughal Empire, New Delhi, 1970.

Khosla, R.P., Administrative structure of the Great Mughals, Delhi, 1991.

Mahalingam T.V., Administration and Social Life under Vijaynagar, Madras, 1940.

Mahajan T.T., Shivaji and his Diplomats, New Delhi, 1991.

Mukerjee Radhakumud, Local Self Government in Ancient India.

P. Saran, The Provincial Government of the Mughals, Bombay, 1973.

Patvardhan M. T. Farsi, Marathi Kosh, Poona, 1925.

Puntambekar S. V., Maratha Polity, 1942.

Qureshi I.H., The Administration of the Sultanate of Delhi, 2nd edition, Lahore, 1944.

Qureshi I.H., The Administration of Mughal Empire, Patna, 1973.

Rangaswami K.V., Aspects of Social and Political System of Manusmriti, Lucknow, 1949.

Sardesai G. S., New History of the Marathas, Vol. I.

Sarkar J.N., Mughal Administration, 1972.

Sen, P.N., The General Principles of Hindu Jurisprudence, Tagore Law Lectures, 1909.

Sen, S.N., Administrative System of the Marathas, Calcutta, Rprt. 1976.

Setu Madhavrao Pagadi, Chhatrapati Shivaji, Poona, 1974.

Shejwalkar T.S., Shri Shivchhatrapati, Bombay, 1964.

Sharma Sri Ram, Mughal Government and Administration, Bombay, 1951.

Tamaskar B.G., The Life and Work of Malik Ambar, Delhi, 1978.

Varad Chariar S., The Hindu Judicial Administration, Lucknow, 1946.

Vaidya C.V., History of Medieval Hindu India, Vols. I to III, Poona, 1924.

Wahed Husain, Administration of Justice during the Muslim Rule in India, Delhi, 1977.

Wilson H.H., A Glossary of Judicial and Revenue Terms, Delhi, 1968.

Journals and Periodicals

Proceedings of Indian History Congress, New Delhi.

Islamic Culture, Hyderabad.

Bharat Itihas Sanshodhak Mandal's Quarterly, Poona.

Itihas Ani Sanskriti, Periodical of Maharashtra State Archives ed. by V.G. Khobrekar.

Samshodhak, V.K. Rajwade's Sanshodhan Mandals, Quarterly, Dhule.

INDEX